The Great Unveiling

The Great Unveiling

W. Graham Scroggie

ZONDERVAN PUBLISHING HOUSE
OF THE ZONDERVAN CORPORATION
GRAND RAPIDS, MICHIGAN 49506

THE GREAT UNVEILING

Grand Rapids, Michigan

Library of Congress Cataloging in Publication Data

Scroggie, William Graham, 1877-1958.
The great unveiling.

1. Bible. N.T. Revelation—Criticism, interpretation, etc.—Addresses, essays, lectures. I. Title.
BS2825.2.S47 228'.06 78-27262
ISBN 0-310-32710-5

Printed in the United States of America

Dedicated
to My Esteemed Friends

Dr. W. H. Griffith Thomas
(Philadelphia)

Dr. G. Campbell Morgan
(Winona Lake)

Dr. James M. Gray
(Chicago)

As a small token of affection for themselves,
and appreciation of their splendid work
in the study and ministry of the Word.

Contents

1. The Human Author of the Book 13
2. The Relations of the Book 21
3. The Chapter Contents of the Book 31
4. The Central Subject of the Book 43
5. The Interpretation of the Apocalypse 55
6. The Application of That Which Is Revealed 73
7. The Historicist: or, Continuously Historical Interpretation 85
8. The Futurist: or, Eschatological Interpretation 99
9. The Structure of the Book 107
10. Syllabus of Studies 119

Foreword

The contents of this volume were delivered as lectures to two congregations over which I had the honor to be pastor, first at Bethesda Free Chapel, Sunderland, England; and then at Charlotte Chapel, Edinburgh, Scotland: and they were delivered without alteration as here given. The number in attendance was large in both places, and a lively interest was maintained throughout a session of some seven months in each case. I mention this to show that there is no need to vulgarize the Bible in order to popularize it; and to express the hope that there may be in our time a great revival of interest in the study of the Word of God on the part alike of pastors and people. If this slender contribution helps in any degree to that end, the writer will feel amply rewarded.

37 Cluny Gardens,
Edinburgh

May, 1925

1
The Human Author of the Book

1
The Human Author of the Book

I. The Home and Occupation of John

A. The Family Circle

Place of their home: Bethsaida (Luke 5:10; John 1:44).

A family of four: Zebedee, Salome, James, John (Mark 1:19, 20; 15:40; Matt. 27:56).

Occupation of father and sons: fishermen (Matt. 4:21).

Character of Salome: ambitious (Luke 8:3; Matt. 20:20).

B. Material Prosperity

Evidence of it: they had hired servants; ministered of their substance; influential in official quarters (Mark 1:20; Matt. 27:56; Luke 8:3; John 19:27; 18:16).

Source of it: the fishing industry very lucrative.

II. The Discipleship and Service-life of John

A. A Follower of John the Baptist (John 1:35, 40): first reference.

B. A Follower of Jesus the Christ: his three calls.

1. **To attachment** (John 1:40).
2. **To discipleship** (Matt. 4:21, 22).
3. **To apostleship** (Luke 6:12-14).

His Relation to Jesus: unique.

1. **One of the first two disciples called** (John 1:35-40).
2. **One of the first four apostles named** (Matt. 4:18-22).

3. **One of the three privileged apostles** (Mark 5:37; Matt. 17:1; 26:37).
4. **One of the four who drew forth our Lord's great prophetic discourse** (Mark 13:3).
5. **One of the two sent to prepare the Passover** (Luke 22:8).
6. **The disciple whom Jesus loved** (John 13:23; 20:2; 21:7, 20).

III. The References to John in the History of the Church

A. The Early References

He appears three times in Acts: in 3:1, at the temple; 4:13, before the council; 8:14, at Samaria.

B. The Last Reference

After Acts 15, we have no further mention of John for forty-five years, and then he names himself indirectly in his Gospel and Epistles, and directly in the Revelation. (Compare John 1:40; Rev. 1:1, 4, 9.)

How is this lack of reference to John to be accounted for?

His retiring disposition? Mary his charge? Destruction of Jerusalem?

IV. The Portrait of John Derived From Tradition

A. His Office and Work

Tradition tells us that John left Jerusalem and went into Asia, perhaps because of the deaths of Peter, Paul, Timothy, Titus, which would leave the Asian churches without a leader. John settled at Ephesus and afterward became bishop there. It is probable he spent the greater part of his later life there, died, and was buried there. His work appears to have been the instruction of the churches, and the appointment of elders.

During this period John was banished to the Island of Patmos, probably by Domitian, A.D. 95 or 96 (but there is weighty evidence for the year A.D. 69); was liberated, probably by Nerva upon his accession, and, it is said, he survived until the reign of Trajan.

Jerome places his death at A.D. 98; others place it years later.

B. Various Incidents

Many stories are told of the aged apostle, and there is no reason to believe that they are spurious. That there is a basis in fact for each of them is likely for they reflect his character as he is represented in the New Testament. For instance:

1. St. John and the Robber

(Told by Clement of Alexandria)

This is the story of a young man whom John entrusted to the Ephesian elder for the care of his soul. The young man got into bad company and ultimately became the leader of a band of brigands. When the apostle returned to Ephesus and asked for his charge, the elder told him that he was dead—to God. John went into the mountains after him and brought him back to Ephesus—and to God.

2. St. John and Cerinthus

Cerinthus was a heretic who taught that the world was not made by God; that Jesus was not born of the Virgin Mary by miraculous conception; that Jesus and Christ were not the same persons; that toward the end of Jesus' ministry the Christ who had come upon Him at His baptism left Him.

Irenaeus preserves the story that "John having entered a bath at Ephesus, and having seen Cerinthus within, went away abruptly, without bathing, saying: 'Let us go lest the house fall, for Cerinthus, the enemy of the Truth, is there.'" (See 2 John 8, 9.)

3. St. John and the Partridge

John Cassian tells a story as follows:

(Found in Hilgenfeld's "Introduction.")

"It is related that the blessed Evangelist John was one day gently caressing a partridge, and that a young man returning from hunting, seeing him thus employed, asked him in amazement how so illustrious a man could give himself up to so trifling an occupation.

"'What dost thou carry in thy hand?' replied John.

"'A bow,' said the youth.

"'Why is it not bent as usual?'

"'Not to take from it, by keeping it constantly bent, the elasticity which it should possess at the moment when I shall shoot my arrow.'

"'Do not be shocked, then, young man, at this brief solace which we allow to our mind, which otherwise losing its spring, could not assist us when necessity requires it.'"

The serenity of John's old age is reflected in this story.

4. St. John and the Church

When at a very advanced age, and too weak to repair to the assemblies of the church, he made the young men carry him thither, and having no longer strength to speak much, he contented himself with saying: "My little children, love one another."

And when asked why he always repeated that one saying, his answer was: "Because it is the Lord's command, and if that be done, enough is done."

Each of these stories is true to John's character and message: (1) and (4) reflect his own love and his teaching on love; (2) reflects his devotion to the truth; and (3) reflects his calm and meditative disposition.

V. The Place of John in the Apostolic Age

A. His Writings and Their Character

One Gospel — Three Epistles

The Revelation

No Scripture was written from about A.D. 68 to A.D. 95. Perhaps the destruction of Jerusalem in A.D. 70 accounts for this.

During this period (1) heresy had time to develop; (2) the number of the apostolic circle was diminishing; (3) the church of this age was not yet fully equipped; (4) much, in the purpose of God, had yet to be added to Holy Scripture; and (5) it was reserved for John to make these final contributions.

The prevailing errors at the close of the first century

were such as affected the person of Christ; Gnostic, Cerinthian, and Docetic heresies. Although it cannot be said that John wrote his Gospel and First Epistle to combat these heresies, yet they stand refuted and condemned in these writings. All John's writings gather around the person of Christ.

The *Gospel* shows that the man of Galilee was God.

The *Epistles* show that it was God who became man.

The *Revelation* shows that ultimate victory is through and for the God-man.

B. His Relation to Peter and Paul

Godet says: "The hour for work had sounded in the first place for Peter. He had founded the Church in Israel, and planted the standard of the new covenant on the ruins of the theocracy.

"Paul had followed. His task had been to liberate the Church from the restrictions of expiring Judaism, and to open the door of the Kingdom of God to the Gentiles.

"John succeeded them, he who was the first to come, and whom his Master reserved to be the last. He completed the fusion of those heterogeneous elements of which the Church had been formed, and he raised Christendom to the relative perfection of which it was then capable.

"It may be said, then, that Peter founded the Primitive Church, Paul emancipated it, and John established it."

VI. The Character of John As Reflected in His Writings

There were two prominent sides to John's character:

A. He was first and last *contemplative.*

His retiring and reticent manner all through his story is evidence of this. Peter is everywhere to the front, but John speaks only three times in his own Gospel. He was not a man of action as was Peter, nor executive as was Paul, but he was essentially contemplative and mystical. His writings bear witness to this. "He does not, like Paul, analyze faith and its object, neither does he argue. It is enough for him to state the Truth, so that everyone who loves it may receive it as he received it, by way of immediate intuition, and not of demonstration. At one bound the heart of John rose to the dazzling height where faith is enthroned."

B. But he was also *passionate.*

Because he was a man of love, it has been thought he tended to be sentimental. Nothing could be more untrue. Look up Luke 9:54; 1 John 2:22; 3:8, 15; 4:20; Mark 3:17. He was incapable of half-enthusiasms and of suspended faith. He was fiery in zeal and severe in temperament. Those opposing elements are quite consistent in one nature. They are reflected in the stories of the Robber and Cerinthus.

It was this man who received the Revelation of Jesus Christ which we are now about to study.

Since both internal and external evidence prove beyond doubt that John the apostle wrote this book (1:1, 4, 9; 22:8), we do not waste a moment's time in examining the subtleties of rationalistic criticism. We find our fellowship with Justin Martyr, Irenaeus, Tertullian, and Origen rather than with the intellects of Tübingen.

2
The Relations of the Book

2
The Relations of the Book

This is a most interesting and important subject. We will consider the relation of this last book of Holy Scripture to the whole Bible, the Old Testament, the New Testament, the Book of Daniel, and the Book of Genesis, respectively.

I. Its Relation to the Whole Bible

The Bible revelation is progressive; from age to age fresh light breaks forth, and the divine program is more widely unfolded.

These Holy Scriptures which separately reveal the progress of revelation, in the aggregate reveal its unity; the many parts go to the making of a sublime whole.

Thus, in Genesis we have Origins, or the beginning of all things.

In Revelation we have Issues, or the end of all things.

And from Exodus to Jude we have Processes, or the way from the beginning to the end.

It has been said that we may estimate the value of a book by trying to imagine what we would do without it.

What would we do without the Revelation? The Bible would be an unfinished story, and that story would seem to set rather in cloud than in glory.

Where there is a starting point, and a track, we naturally expect to find a goal; but without the Revelation there would be no goal.

Dr. Griffith Thomas has outlined the Bible in this way:

Genesis to Deuteronomy
Revelation
Joshua to Esther
Preparation
Job to Song of Solomon
Aspiration
Isaiah to Malachi
Expectation
Matthew to John
Manifestation
Acts to Jude
Realization
The Apocalypse
Consummation

There we see again the relation of the last book of the Bible to all the rest, and its vital importance. Revelation at the beginning, and through all its stages, works inevitably toward a consummation, and that consummation is prophetically unveiled in this last book. Whether or not the book was the last to be written, its only possible place is last because of its contents. Place any other book of the Bible last, and you would have an anticlimax.

The Revelation is, then, an issue, a goal, a consummation in relation to all the other Scriptures.

II. Its Relation to the Old Testament

If there were no Old Testament, there could be no understanding of the Apocalypse, for the symbolism of this book is not Greek, nor Roman, but Jewish. It is pervaded with the style and imagery of the Old Testament, and is molded by the historical and prophetical books.

On this subject, Prof. Milligan, the elder, says: "The Book is absolutely steeped in the memories, the incidents, the thoughts, and the language of the Church's past. (By 'Church,' Milligan means Israel, though we would not have so spoken of them.) To such an extent is this the case that it must be doubted whether it contains a single figure not drawn from the Old Testament, or a single complete sentence not more or less built up of materials brought from the same source.

"It is a perfect mosaic of passages from the Old Testament, at one time quoted verbally, at another referred to by distinct allusion; now taken from one scene in Jewish history, and now again from two or three together."

Professor Marvin Vincent, whose view this is also, has started us on the line of an altogether fascinating subject. Follow these suggestions:

The heresy of the Nicolaitanes is the heresy of Balaam (2:14).

The evil in the church of Thyatira is personified in Jezebel (2:20).

The angelic captain in the war against the dragon is the Michael of Daniel (12:7).

Jerusalem, Mount Zion, Babylon, the Euphrates, Sodom, and Egypt are symbols of the holy bliss of the saints, of the transgressors against God, and the judgment of the wicked (21:2; 14:1; 16:19; 9:14; 11:8).

The battle of Armageddon carries us back to the great slaughters in the plain of Megiddo (Judges 5:19; Ps. 83:9; 2 Kings 23:29).

The promises to the churches are given under the figure of the tree of life, the hidden manna, the white stone, the iron scepter, the morning star, the pillar in the temple of God (2:7, 17, 27, 28; 3:5, 12, 20).

Heaven is described under the image of the tabernacle in the wilderness (11:1, 19; 6:9; 8:3; 4:6).

The plagues of chapter 8 are the plagues of Egypt.

The crossing of the Red Sea and the destruction of Korah are blended in the representation of the deliverance of God's people (12:15, 16).

Of the prophets, Haggai refers to the earthquake of chapter 6; and Joel speaks of the sun changing into the blackness of sackcloth and the moon into blood; Isaiah the falling stars, the fig tree casting her untimely fruit, and the heavens departing like a scroll; Ezekiel the scorpions of chapter 9, the description of the new Jerusalem in chapter 21, the roll in chapter 5, and the little book in chapter 10; Zechariah the opening of the seals in chapter 6, and the olive trees in chapter 11.

The vision of the glorified Redeemer (1:12-20) is combined

from Exodus, Zechariah, Daniel, Ezekiel, Isaiah, and the Psalms.

These are only a few of the parallels which can be found in comparing the Old Testament with the Book of Revelation. "Out of a total number of 404 verses in this Book about 265 verses contain Old Testament language, and about 550 references are made to Old Testament passages," a fact significant enough.

This feature of Revelation is not only of great interest, but also of the profoundest importance as we shall see when we come to the subject of interpretation, for it means that the understanding of Scripture is possible to those who cannot lay claim to a wide knowledge in other fields.

Remember then, that without the Old Testament the Apocalypse would be a hopeless enigma, and that without the Apocalypse the Old Testament would be an unfinished story. That is their relation.

III. Its Relation to the New Testament

Each Testament is divided into three similar parts—the Old Testament into history (Genesis to Esther), philosophy (Job to Song of Solomon), and prophecy (Isaiah to Malachi); and the New Testament into history (Matthew to Acts), doctrine (Romans to Jude), and prophecy (Revelation).

We have already seen that the Apocalypse is the crown or goal of the whole. But regard it now only in its relation to the completion of the three parts named. The subject of the first part is, *the Christ;* of the second, *the church;* and of the third, *the consummation.*

All these subjects are gathered up and completed in the third of these parts:

Revelation 1	The Christ
Revelation 2–3	The Church
Revelation 4–22	The Consummation

So that, once again, without this book the New Testament would be an unfinished story.

In the Old Testament we see that which is earthly.

In the Acts and the Epistles we see that which is heavenly.

In the Gospels both meet in Christ.

And in the Apocalypse we have a small Bible in which again

the earthly and the heavenly meet in Christ; so that the book is the climax and completion of each of the Testaments, and of the whole Bible. But it bears a special relation also to some of the separate books of the Bible. So now consider:

IV. Its Relation to the Book of Daniel

The Book of Daniel is the Apocalypse of the Old Testament, and the Apocalypse is the Daniel of the New Testament. These books are intimately related and neither can be rightly studied without the other.

It is important to know exactly what their relation is.

They both treat of the same period, but the horizon of Daniel is much wider than that of John; and that is natural for Daniel had 700 years before him which John had behind him.

Yet in another view, John's horizon is much wider than Daniel's, because while the latter treats only of things on *earth,* the former treats also of things in *heaven;* and while Daniel keeps within the field of *time,* John carries us into *eternity.*

In other words, there is ground which is common to them both, but Daniel began before John, and John continued after Daniel, that is to say, as to subject.

The point may be illustrated in this way:

DANIEL	REVELATION

The enclosed part represents the common ground, the lines, the ground peculiar to each.

The situation may be illustrated also in this way:

DANIEL	REVELATION
Treats of four empires *Babylonian* *Medo-Persian* *Grecian* *Roman*	Treats of one empire *Roman*
Whole course of Roman empire in summary.	Latter end of Roman empire in detail.
Things on earth.	Things on earth and in heaven.
Jews / Gentiles.	Church / Jews / Gentiles.
Ends with the Millennium.	Goes on into the eternal state.

Across the centuries the captive in Babylon and the captive on Patmos join hands, and their voices blend as they tell of judgment and of victory.

We must consider the Apocalypse further, and finally in

V. Its Relation to the Book of Genesis

Between these two books, the first and the last, there is the closest connection, by way of comparison and contrast. The following will set the student along a most profitable line of investigation:

A. Comparison

Genesis	Revelation
God	God
First heaven and earth	Last heaven and earth
First rest	Final rest
Paradise lost	Paradise regained
The tree and the river	The tree and the river
Husband and wife	The Lamb and the bride

B. Contrast

Genesis	Revelation
Satan victorious	Satan defeated
Judgment pronounced	Judgment executed
The divine face hidden	We shall see His face
The curse pronounced	The curse removed
The gates shut against us	The gates are never shut
Death overtook all men	There is no more death
All faces wet with tears	All tears wiped away
Terror came with the night	No terror because no night
Banished from the Tree of Life	We have a right to the Tree of Life
Exiles from the earthly garden	Inheritors of the heavenly city
The cherubim keeping man out	The cherubim welcoming man in

These and many other contrasts and comparisons may be found in these two wonderful books. They stand in relation to one another as foundation stone to capstone, and all the rest of Scripture is the superstructure in between.

Revelation, then, is a Book to be studied. The neglect of it is an affront to God, because it implies either that the book is not worth studying, or that it is impossible to know what it means. Yet it is sadly and widely neglected.

Some reasons why the Apocalypse should be specially studied:

1. Because it is a revelation, an unveiling.
2. Because special blessing is promised to those who read and obey.
3. Because without it the Bible cannot be properly understood.
4. Because it is all about Christ.
5. Because it reaches further on than any other book in the Bible.
6. Because the symbolism of the book is biblical.
7. Because it discloses to us the ultimate triumph of right in its age-long conflict with wrong.

3
The Chapter Contents of the Book

3
The Chapter Contents of the Book

Each chapter should be read repeatedly with this summary before you, which we will later amplify.

I. Alpha

John the apostle was banished to the isle called Patmos "for the Word of God, and for the testimony of Jesus" (v. 9). There he received a revelation "to write" (vv. 11, 19), a revelation which would bring special blessing to the obedient reader (v. 3). This revelation was addressed to "seven churches" in Asia Minor (v. 4), and was prophetic in character (vv. 1, 7). Christ is the central figure in the unveiling (vv. 12-16), and is seen in relation both to the saved (vv. 13, 20) and the unsaved (v. 7). John was overcome by what he had seen and heard (v. 17), but was reassured and strengthened for his ministry (vv. 17, 18).

II.-III. Churches

The apostle, in obedience to the command (1:11), writes to each of seven churches in Asia Minor a message from the risen Lord (1:18). The churches were at Ephesus; Smyrna; Pergamum; Thyatira; Sardis; Philadelphia; and Laodicea. In chapter 2 we find the letters to the first four churches, and in chapter 3 to the remaining three. Each of these epistles has its own features, yet all of them follow a similar plan. Broadly, the plan is (1) an address; (2) a revelation of the Speaker; (3) a declaration of His knowledge; (4) a description of the church's state, with praise or warning as the case requires; (5) a reference to Christ's coming again; (6) a universal command to hear; and (7) a special promise to the overcomer. What the Spirit says to each of the churches He says to them all (2:7, 11, 17, 29; 3:6, 13, 22).

IV. Thrones

A door is opened in heaven (v. 1) and John is caught up in the Spirit to see "things which must be hereafter" (vv. 1, 2). He saw a throne on which God sat (v. 2), and encircling the throne was a rainbow (v. 3). Round about God's throne were twenty-four other thrones on which as many crowned elders sat (v. 4). In addition, there were present "seven spirits" (v. 5) and "four living creatures" which are described (vv. 6-8). These creatures, together with the elders, praise and worship God, and sing a great creation song (vv. 9-11).

V. Lion-Lamb

God on the throne held a sealed book in His hand (v. 1), which no one was able or worthy to open, all heaven, and earth, and hell having been challenged by a strong angel (vv. 2, 3). On this account John was very upset (v. 4). Whereupon one of the elders consoled him by announcing that "the Lion of the tribe of Juda" was both worthy and able to open the seals (v. 5). He then saw the Lamb of God—once slain, but now in the midst of the throne and its surrounding life—go and take the book out of the hand of God (vv. 6, 7); whereupon the living creatures and the elders fell down before Him and sang a great redemption song (vv. 8-10). This song was followed by a doxology in which thousands of angels united with the creatures and elders (vv. 11, 12); and this doxology swelled into another, in which all creation joined in worship of the Lamb (vv. 13, 14).

VI. Seals

The opening of the seven-sealed book now begins. Those things which lay under the first four seals were commanded to "come," or "go," by the four living creatures respectively (vv. 1-8). Also under each of these four seals a horse is seen—white, red, black, and pale respectively. Under the first seal a conqueror goes forth (vv. 1, 2); under the second, peace is taken from the earth (vv. 3, 4); under the third, famine is announced (vv. 5, 6); and under the fourth, a quarter of the earth is killed by sword, famine, pestilence,and wild beasts (vv. 7, 8). In this chapter two more seals are loosed. Under the fifth are seen beneath the altar in the heavenly temple those who for faithfulness to Christ had been slain, and they are heard calling upon their sovereign Lord to avenge their blood upon their murderers (vv. 9, 10). In reply they are clothed in white and are bidden be patient until the full complement of the martyrs was fulfilled (v. 11). Under the sixth seal there was a great earthquake; sun, moon, and stars, heaven and earth are embraced in the fearful convulsion (vv. 12-14). All classes of society are stricken with terror, and in vain seek refuge from the wrath of the Lamb (vv. 15-17).

VII. Multitude

The previous chapter ended with the question, "Who is able to stand?" Here we have the answer (v. 9). Four angels are seen ready to hurt the earth, the sea, and trees, but "another angel" from the East forbids them to do this until the servants of God have been sealed in their foreheads (vv. 1-3). The sealed are all Israelites, twelve thousand of every tribe—one hundred and forty-four thousand in all. For their idolatry Dan and Ephraim are omitted from the list, and Levi and Joseph take their places (vv. 4-8). "After these things" John saw "a great multitude" of redeemed Gentiles (v. 9) standing "before the throne and before the Lamb," singing a salvation song (v. 10). Also, all the angels of heaven are prostrating themselves before the throne and worshiping God in a benediction song (vv. 11, 12). One of the elders asked John who he thought those were who stood in white before God, and where they had come from (v. 13). This same elder then tells John that these are saved people who suffered during "the great tribulation," who, having come out of it, are now "before the throne of God," serving Him in the temple (vv. 14, 15). Their heavenly position is contrasted with their once earthly lot (vv. 16, 17).

VIII. Trumpets

The seventh seal is now opened, but before the judgments under it are poured forth there is a short period of "silence in heaven," during which an angel who was standing by the golden altar of prayer added much incense to the prayers of the saints which are represented as on the altar, and these prayers, together with the smoke of the incense, went "up before God." Then the angel, taking the censer, filled it with the fire of the altar, and cast it into the earth; and there followed the evidences of coming judgment (vv. 1-5).

Then seven angels, holding seven trumpets, prepared themselves to sound (v. 6).

This chapter contains the sounding of four of these trumpets, and a prophecy of the three terrible woes to follow.

The instruments of the first judgment are hail, fire, and blood; and its issue, the smiting of the earth (v. 7).

The instrument of the second judgment is a mountain-ball of fire; and its issue the smiting of the sea (vv. 8, 9).

The instrument of the third judgment is a great burning star; and its issue is the smiting of the waters (vv. 10, 11).

The instrument of the fourth judgment is not named, but its issue is the smiting of the sun, moon, and stars (v. 12).

The damage done by these judgments respectively is of a third part of the spheres visited (vv. 7-12).

Then John saw, flying in mid-heaven, an eagle which "with a loud voice" announced the three remaining trumpets as "woe" judgments (v. 13).

IX. Locusts

The fifth trumpet is now sounded, which is the first "woe" judgment. A star fell from heaven to earth, and there was given to the angel the key of the abyss, which he opened. So great a smoke arose out of the pit that the sun was obscured by it, and out of the smoke locusts came forth upon the earth (vv. 1-3). These locusts are commissioned (vv. 4, 5), and the time of their stay appointed (v. 5). Also they are minutely described (vv. 7-10), and the effect on men of their presence is stated (v. 6). They have a king over them whose name is given in Hebrew and Greek (v. 11). The sixth trumpet, or second "woe," is now announced (v. 12).

From the golden altar a voice commanded that the four angels which were restrained in the East should be loosed (vv. 13, 14). They were appointed to kill the third part of men (v. 15). The army of angelic horsemen engaged in this judgment numbered 200,000,000 (v. 16). The horses are described (vv. 17,

19), and by the fire, smoke, and brimstone which went out of their mouths was a third of the men killed (vv. 17, 18). But, notwithstanding this judgment, the remaining two-thirds of the men did not repent of their many sins (vv. 20, 21).

X. Book

John saw a strong angel come down from heaven and he described him (v. 1). He stood on sea and land, and cried with a lion-like voice, after which seven thunders spoke (vv. 2, 3). The apostle, who was about to write what the thunders had uttered, was commanded not to do so (v. 4). The great angel then swore by God the Creator (vv. 5, 6) that there should be delay no longer, but that the divine vengeance would now at last be fully poured out upon the wicked (vv. 6, 7). John was then commanded to take from the hand of the "great angel" a little book, and to eat it (vv. 8, 9), which, when he did it, was in his mouth sweet, but in his belly bitter (vv. 9, 10).

XI. Witnesses

The inner parts of the temple at Jerusalem are to be measured, but not the outer courts (vv. 1, 2).

God has in the Holy City at this time two witnesses who for three-and-a-half years bear Him testimony (vv. 3, 7). Miraculous powers are granted them, and those who attempt to injure them are killed (vv. 5, 6). At the end of this period they are slain, and for three-and-a-half days their bodies lie unburied in Jerusalem (vv. 7-9). The earth rejoices to have gotten rid of them (v. 10), but God raises them to life and translates them to heaven in the presence of their enemies (vv. 11, 12). A great earthquake then shakes the city, and much damage is done to life and property (v. 13).

The third "woe" is now introduced (v. 14), and the issues of it are anticipated in the songs heard in heaven, songs which celebrate the coming victory of Christ, and judgment of the wicked (vv. 15-18).

Then are seen and heard the usual precursors of judgment (v. 19).

XII. Dragon

In heaven there were two great signs—a woman about to

bring forth a child, and a dragon waiting to devour it when it was born. This dragon and his power are described (vv. 1-4). A man-child was brought forth and was caught up to heaven, and the woman fled into the wilderness for twelve hundred and sixty days, where she was nourished by God (vv. 5, 6).

War in heaven. Michael and his angels attacked the dragon and his angels (vv. 7, 8), with the result that the latter were cast down to the earth (v. 9). A voice in heaven now proclaims that the triumph of Christ and of His suffering saints is at hand, and bids the heavens rejoice (vv. 7-12). The same voice pronounces woe upon the earth on account of the devil's having gone to it (v. 12).

The cause of the woman's flight is revealed (vv. 13, 14) where she went (v. 14), for what period of time (v. 14), how she was pursued by the dragon, and how she was helped to escape are here set forth (vv. 15, 16). The dragon now determines war upon her seed, and goes away to prepare it (v. 17; 13:1), by bringing to manifestation the two wild beasts.

XIII. Beasts

The first beast comes up out of the sea, and combines the features of a leopard, a bear, and a lion. He has ten crowned horns and seven blasphemous heads, and he derives his power from the dragon. All the earth worships the beast (v. 4), who waxes bold in blasphemy against God and His people, and continues to do so for forty-two months (vv. 5, 6). He makes war with the saints, and overcomes them, and he is given universal authority (vv. 7, 8).

The second beast comes up out of the earth. He has two horns, and speaks like a dragon (v. 11). He is subordinate to the first beast, and causes the world to worship him (v. 12). He works miracles whereby all the earth is deceived (vv. 13, 14). An image of the first beast is made, and the power of speech is given to it, and power to cause them to be killed who do not worship it (v. 15). Furthermore, this second beast imposes a trademark upon all people, without which no one is allowed to do business. The first beast is a man, and his number is 666.

XIV. Angels

On Mount Zion are seen the Lamb, and with Him 144,000 sealed ones (v. 1), who have been purchased out of the earth (v. 3), and who are the "first-fruits" from among men unto God and the Lamb (v. 4). They are heard singing before the throne a song which they only could learn (vv. 2, 3).

An angel is seen flying in mid-heaven proclaiming to all men that divine judgment is come, and imploring them to worship God the Creator (vv. 6, 7).

A second angel follows announcing the fall of Babylon (v. 8).

A third angel in solemn tones warns men against worshiping the beast, or receiving his trademark, and declares what will be the portion of those who do (vv. 9-12). In these days they are called "blessed" who die in the Lord (v. 13).

An angel from the temple announces that the harvest of the earth is overripe, and bids one "like unto a son of man" send forth his sickle, which he does, and the earth is reaped (vv. 14-16).

Another angel is seen with a sharp sickle, and is bidden gather the vintage of the earth, which, when gathered, was cast into the winepress of God's wrath (vv. 17-20).

XV. Wrath

Those who "come victorious from the beast" are seen beyond the tribulation, and they sing the song of Moses and of the Lamb, the words of which are given (vv. 2-4).

Seven angels are seen in heaven, to whom one of the living creatures gives seven plagues, "the last," in which "is filled up the wrath of God" (v. 1)

The temple is filled with the smoke of glory and power, so that none can enter it until these plagues have been poured out (vv. 5-8).

XVI. Bowls

The angels are asked to empty their bowls (v. 1).

The first bowl is poured into the earth, and becomes a noisome sore upon the worshipers of the beast (v. 2).

The second bowl is poured into the sea, which becomes blood, so that all in it died (v. 3).

The third bowl is poured into all drinking waters, and the waters become blood (v. 4). The angel vindicates the justice of this plague, for the peoples had shed the blood of the saints, and now are given blood to drink (vv. 5, 6). Heaven endorses this verdict (v. 7).

The fourth bowl is poured out upon the sun, and it scorches man with great heat, so that they blaspheme the divine name, and do not repent of their iniquities (vv. 8, 9).

The fifth bowl is poured out upon the throne of the beast, whose kingdom is darkened, and whose subjects suffer fearful pains, yet do not repent of their works (vv. 10, 11).

The sixth bowl is poured out upon the Euphrates, which becomes dry, so that a way is made for the kings of the East to come West (v. 12).

At this juncture John saw three unclean spirits from the mouth of the dragon, beast, and false prophet go forth throughout the earth to gather its kings unto the great battle of Armageddon (vv. 13-16).

And the seventh bowl is poured out upon the air, accompanied by a voice and physical phenomena (vv. 17, 18). The effect of this judgment is the fall of cities, among which Babylon comes in for special notice (v. 19). A great and heavy hail falls from heaven upon men so that they blaspheme God (vv. 20, 21).

XVII. Woman

At the instigation of an angel John is carried into a wilderness, where he beholds a woman sitting upon a scarlet-colored beast. She holds a foul cup in her hand, and has an inscription upon her forehead. And she is drunk with the blood of the saints (vv. 1-6). John greatly wonders at what he beholds, whereupon the angel promises to explain to him the mystery (v. 7), which he did. The beast was, and is not, yet shall come (vv. 8, 9). The seven heads and ten horns are seven and ten kings respectively, who are all in agreement with, and assist the beast (vv. 10-13). These war against the Lamb, but are overthrown (v. 14). The waters on which the woman is are peoples (vv. 1, 15). The woman is to be destroyed by the beast upon which she sits (v. 3), and by the ten kings (vv. 12, 16), for God will put it into their hearts to give their kingdom to the beast. This woman "is that great city, which reigneth over the kings of the earth" (v. 18).

XVIII. Babylon

A great angel from heaven announces the fall of Babylon, and the reason for it (vv. 1-3). God bids His people come out of her, and so escape her plagues. Babylon's sins are recounted, her speedy ruin proclaimed, and the effect of her fall upon those who trafficked with her is declared (vv. 4-19). Saints, apostles, and prophets are invited to rejoice over her overthrow (v. 20). A strong angel, to indicate how sudden and complete would be the fall of Babylon, takes up a great stone and casts it into the sea, saying, "Thus with violence shall that great city Babylon be thrown down, and shall be found no more at all" (v. 21). Her career is at an end because of her sins (vv. 22-24).

XIX. Suppers

"After these things" the apostle hears the song of the great multitude in heaven celebrating the judgment of the harlot (vv. 1-3). The elders and living creatures support this song (v. 4). The multitude then praises God that the marriage of the Lamb is come (vv. 5-8) and John is asked to write that they are blessed who are invited to it (v. 9).

He then sees heaven opened, and Christ comes forth to war. He sits upon a white horse, and His appearance is described (vv. 11-13). With Him are the armies of heaven, and He comes forth to smite and to rule, and He is King of Kings and Lord of Lords (vv. 14-16).

An angel summons all the birds of the sky to come to the great supper of God, and eat the flesh of the mighty of the earth (vv. 17, 18).

The beast and the false prophet are then taken and cast into the lake of fire; the wicked are slain by the sword of Christ, and the birds eat their flesh (vv. 19-21).

XX. Millennium

An angel binds Satan and casts him into the abyss for a thousand years (vv. 1-3), and those who had been faithful to Christ are given thrones of judgment, and they reign with Him throughout the Millennium (vv. 4-6).

At the end of that time Satan is to be loosed, and shall go forth and deceive all the earth, gathering men together to make war upon Jerusalem and the saints (vv. 7-9), but these hosts are destroyed by fire, and the devil is cast into the lake of fire (vv. 9, 10).

A great white throne is then set up, before which the spiritually dead are judged, and these with death and Hades, are cast into the lake of fire (vv. 11-15).

XXI. Holy City

The New Jerusalem is seen to descend out of heaven prepared as a bride for her husband. With its descent God comes to tabernacle with men, to banish sorrow and death, and to make all things new (vv. 1-5). The portions of the faithful and sinners respectively is announced (vv. 5-8).

The Holy City is now minutely described, and its glories portrayed (vv. 9-21).

God and the Lamb are the temple and the light of the city (vv. 22, 23). Its gates are never shut, and kings bring the glory and honor of the nations into it, into which nothing unclean can enter (vv. 24-27).

XXII. Advent

Description of the city continued. A river proceeds out of the throne, and runs through the midst of the street. By the river the tree of life bears its fruits (vv. 1, 2). There is no night and no curse, but all is blessedness, with the Lamb in the midst (vv. 3-5).

A blessing is again pronounced on them who keep the prophecy of this book (vv. 6, 7). John would have worshiped the angel through whom the revelation had been made, but he forbade him (vv. 8, 9); and commanded him to seal up the words of the prophecy (vv. 10, 11).

The Alpha and Omega announces His speedy advent to reward every man according to his work (vv. 12-15). It is Jesus who has sent forth this revelation for the sake of the churches (v. 16). There is further invitation and warning, and another declaration of the speedy coming of the Lord Jesus (vv. 16-21).

4
The Central Subject of the Book

4
The Central Subject of the Book

In 1522 Luther wrote of the Revelation, "My spirit cannot adapt itself to the Book, and a sufficient reason why I do not esteem it highly is that Christ is neither taught nor recognized in it." We find that twelve years later he had modified that view. Yet to the end he remained doubtful about its apostolicity. How a man of Luther's intelligence in the Scriptures could make such a statement as the above baffles understanding, for if there is one book more than another in the Bible whose subject is Christ, that book is the Revelation.

The opening words strike the keynote of the book, and are its true title: "The Revelation (Apocalypse) of Jesus Christ."

As to the meaning of these words there is some difference of opinion. Do they mean that the book is

(a) An unveiling of Himself, as when a statue is unveiled? or,

(b) An unveiling concerning Him wherein God makes Him known? or,

(c) An unveiling by Him, that is, a revelation of the future which God gave Him to give to us?

The last two interpretations are certainly true. It is an unveiling of the future by Christ, but as the future is entirely bound up in Him, it is also necessarily an unveiling concerning Him. It is therefore "the Revelation of and by Jesus Christ."

In all evolution the movement is from the simple to the complex, and that should also characterize the study of this book. We must not begin with what is mysterious—the seals, the trumpets, the bowls, and so forth—but with what is perfectly plain, the revelation of Christ, and if we had loved Him better we would have seen and understood Him more in this book. Learn first of all what may be definitely known, and then approach the things about which we may not be able to arrive at so clear an understanding. Take up the book, therefore, and read it for what there is of Christ in it.

We shall divide our study into five sections—the Unveilings, the Utterances, the Revelations, the Activities, and the Triumphs of Christ.

I. The Unveilings of Christ

The reference here is to what He is rather than to *where* He is, or *what* He does. There are some twenty-five names or titles given to our Lord in the Revelation, and as the field of inquiry is a rich one, let us look in turn for the Personal, the Official, and the Dispensational Unveilings.

A. The Personal Unveiling of Christ

Here we must search out those names which reveal to us one or other of the many aspects of the divine nature, and what our Lord is in Himself and in His relation to men. Of these there are about a dozen, some telling of His deity, some of His humanity, and some combining these ideas.

1. **His Deity**
   He is:
   God and the Almighty in 1:8.
   The Son of God in 2:18.
   The Lord in 15:4.
   The Holy One in 16:5.
   The Word of God in 19:13.
   The Amen (or True One) in 3:14.
2. **His Humanity**
   He is:
   The Son of man in 1:13.
   Jesus in 14:12.
   Jesus Christ in 1:1.
3. **The God-Man**
   He is:
   The Lord Jesus in 22:20.
   The Lord Jesus Christ in 22:21.

The doctrines implied in these various names are many and profound. They tell:

Of the co-equality of the Son with the Father;

Of His holiness as essential and not derived;

Of His being Eternal Truth, and not merely knowing, or speaking it;

Of His taking upon Himself human nature;

And of the redeeming sacrifice and attainment to sovereign Lordship through death.

We should therefore worship Him who is here revealed.

Search out also in this book—

B. The Official Unveiling of Christ

Those titles tell what our Lord becomes to, and does for men, rather than of what He is in Himself.

For instance:

He is the Christ in 11:15; 12:10; 20:4, 6; the Messiah, the anointed of God for the fulfillment of a divine mission.

He is the Faithful and True Witness in 3:14, with reference most probably to what is declared in this book.

He is the King in 15:3; 17:14; 19:16, which title tells of His coming world dominion, and of the realization ideally of the principle of monarchy.

And He is the Master, or Despotes, in 6:10, the sovereign Lord and disposer of the whole earth.

And then, there is what, for lack of a more comprehensive word, we may call

C. The Dispensational Unveiling of Christ

The titles which we place under this classification are symbolical and philosophical, and express our Lord's relation comprehensively to time and things, with special reference, in instances to redemption.

Look, for example, at the three titles in 22:13.

Christ is the Alpha and Omega. These are the first and last letters of the Greek alphabet, and carry with them the suggestion of literature, and here might signify the literature of revelation; the Bible, of which Christ is the entire substance: that which lies between its first and last letters.

He is also the First and the Last, a title which seems to carry the idea of history, and thus would mean that Christ was the inclusive man, the perfect manhood, the crown of all history.

And further, He is called the beginning and the end, which appears to have reference to creation and time, so that He is at the poles of time, and is the cause, maintainer, and perfecter of creation. These titles are fathomless.

He is called the first begotten in 1:5, with reference to His resurrection.

The Lamb in 5:6, and twenty-six other times in the book, is a title which speaks of redemption, and takes us back to the Passover in Egypt.

He is the Lion of the tribe of Judah, a figure which tells of royalty and carries us back to the blessing of Jacob upon Judah, through which tribe it was promised the messianic King should come (Gen. 49:9, 10).

In this book Christ is also called the root and the offspring of David in 22:16, meaning that He was both before and after David, from whom David came, and who came from David, the producer and the product. This is a dispensational title, as will at once be evident.

He is also the Morning Star in 22:16, indicating that He vouchsafes and ushers in the eternal day.

By so many names and titles is our blessed Lord unveiled in this book to those who have eyes to see, and seeing, we can only unite with the elders, the living creatures, and the angelic hosts to praise and worship the Lamb.

II. The Utterances of Christ

A. The Passages

It is not always easy, when there are as many speakers as in this book, to say which are the words of our Lord, and which the words of angels. But there appear to be eighteen paragraphs of His words, although of two of them there may be some doubt.

They are as follows:

1. 1:8
2. 1:11
3. 1:17-20
4. 2:1-7
5. 2:8-11
6. 2:12-17
7. 2:18-28
8. 3:1-6
9. 3:7-13
10. 3:14-22

11. 11:1-3 (?)
12. 16:15
13. 18:4, 5 (?)
14. 22:7
15. 22:12, 13
16. 22:16
17. 22:18, 19
18. 22:20

It will be observed that only three of these paragraphs are in the body of the book (and two of these are doubtful), and that all the others (fifteen) are at the beginning and the end. In a very literal sense, therefore, Christ is the Alpha and Omega of the Apocalypse.

B. The Teaching

But how rich and full is the revelation of our Lord and His purposes in these passages.

He speaks to us of:

His Divine Person (1:8): "The Lord God."

His Voluntary Sacrifice (1:18): "I became dead."

His Sovereign Lordship (1:18): "I have the keys of death and of Hades."

His Inclusive Knowledge (chs. 2 and 3): "I know," repeated seven times.

His Perfect Justice (22:12): "To render to each man according as his work is."

His Absolute Authority (22:16): "I have sent mine angel."

His Second Advent (22:7, 12, 20): "Behold, I come quickly."

The whole book gathers around Him, as we have seen, but the words which He Himself speaks are especially emphatic and impressive.

C. The Standpoint

This is especially true when we realize that they were spoken from heaven. We have been asked to believe that, great as Christ's utterances were on earth, they must not be regarded as infallible utterances. Were that idea true, we should have been able to contrast His postresurrection with His preresurrection teaching. But the simple fact is that what Christ said during the forty days of His manifestation after the cross, and what He afterward said from heaven is in perfect accord with all that He said before, only confirming and extending its meaning. Heaven, then, is the standpoint of this entire revelation.

III. The Relations of Christ

His relation to time should be noted. We have already remarked on the significance of the titles Alpha and Omega, First and Last, Beginning and End.

But He further speaks of Himself as the One "who is (present) and who was (past), and who is to come (future), the same yesterday, and to-day, and for ever."

We read of "The Lamb slain from the foundation of the world" (13:8); of the "man child" which the woman brought forth (12:5); and of Him who "loosed us from our sins by his blood" (1:5); referring to what is past.

Again, we read that He is on His Father's throne (3:21); that He has sovereign power (1:18); that He beholds and estimates the conduct of His people (2:3), which passages have reference to the present.

We also read that He will visit the wicked with judgments (5:5);

Will establish His throne on the earth (20:10);

Will bring those who trust in Him to everlasting blessedness (7:15-17), and much besides, all which is yet future.

So Christ is related to all time, and specifically to its several ages.

Christ's moral relations should also be traced in this book. Here we may note

A. His Relation to Heaven

1. To the Father.

It is a significant fact that only once in the book does God speak directly (21:5-8); yet the whole revelation is from Him.

"The Revelation of Jesus Christ
which God gave him" (1:1).

The Father is throughout vindicating the Son, and the Son is throughout glorifying the Father. They are one in essence, for they each claim to be "the Alpha and Omega" (1:8; 21:6); they are also one in purpose.

2. To the Spirit.

The third person of the Holy Trinity is mentioned thirteen times in the Apocalypse and is everywhere seen to be "the executive of the godhead." The majority of the references are in chapters 2 and 3, where Christ identifies Himself with the Spirit, for He says: "Let him hear what the Spirit saith to the churches," although He Himself is the speaker throughout.

3. To unfallen angels.

Angels crowd the stage of the Apocalypse and are seen everywhere speaking and acting on behalf of God and of Christ. So intimate is the relation between them that, as we have seen, it is difficult in places to know where the angel's words end, and Christ's begin. See, for example, 11:1-3; 18:4-20; 22:6, 7, 10-15. Christ is the Lord of Hosts, and here we may behold His angelic hosts,

> Who post o'er land and ocean without rest:
> They also serve who only stand and wait.

B. His Relation to Hell

If the visions of this book are bright with the pinions of unfallen angels, they are also dark with the wings of the fallen. There are the "three unclean spirits" of 16:13, 14, and the unnumbered demons of 18:2. And throughout the book we see the dark shadow of the devil. The relation of Christ to these, and their relation to Christ is quite clear. They are deadly antagonistic, seen working through agents, and battling for the ultimate mastery.

C. His Relation to Earth

The individual element in the Apocalypse is prominent. All sorts of persons move to and fro. There are the bad, such as the beast and the false prophet; and the good, such as the two witnesses, the 144,000 sealed ones, and others.

The relation of Christ to these, and all whom they represent, is according to their character. We see Him standing by His people in the fires of affliction, and ultimately delivering them. And we see Him pouring out His judgments upon the unrepentant wicked, and ultimately destroying them.

Thus, our Lord is presented at the end of the New Testament as at the beginning, in His relation to heaven (see Matt. 1), and to earth (see Matt. 2:3), and to hell (see Matt. 4:1-11), and He stands related to each as sovereign Lord.

IV. The Activities of Christ

I have said that Christ and the devil act through agents, the saints, and the wicked respectively. It is well, then, to remember who the real actors are. There are here three classes of persons in relation to whom Christ is active.

A. THE CHURCH—WHICH HE IS CHASTENING

The churches of chapters 2 and 3 are pictures of the church, and there can be no mistaking that Christ acts in relation to them. Throughout He declares that He will come, and what He will do; and He represents Himself as now "Walking in the midst of the seven golden lampstands." He is imminent and acting in His church in every place and throughout the age, and the work is one of chastening and perfecting.

B. ISRAEL—WHICH HE IS RESTORING

He who once was so active in the chosen nation, but who for so long has assumed a passive attitude, is once again, according to many Scriptures in both Testaments, to resume His dealings with it and fulfill His covenants of promise. This book furnishes evidence of His purpose.

There is the sealing of 144,000 Jews, in chapter 7;

The two witnesses, almost certainly Jews, in chapter 11;

The mother of the man-child in chapter 12, who surely is Israel, and who, fleeing from the persecutor, is nourished by God in the wilderness for three and a half years.

There is also the reference to the "twelve tribes of the children of Israel" in chapter 21, who have their part in the Holy City, the New Jerusalem.

And the fact that the great battle of Armageddon is to be fought in Palestine is evidence of a coming special activity of the Messiah in Israel, an activity which shall have as its end their restoration for the fulfillment of age-long purpose.

C. THE WORLD—WHICH HE IS JUDGING

The Apocalypse is a book of world movements, and whether it be blessing or judgment, all is traceable to Christ; He is the great Factor behind the visible. In relation to the world we see His activity in judgment in chapters 6; 8; 9; 14; 16–19, and in grace in chapters 7; 20–22. As all men are included in His purposes, all are within the compass of His activities, which are characterized throughout by judgment, now condemning, and now justifying.

V. The Triumphs of Christ

These triumphs consist in all that has gone before, in His unveilings, utterances, relations, and activities. Nowhere are the true character of evil, and its terrible powers, more fully displayed than in this book, but nowhere are the power and glory of Christ more fully revealed. In all these scenes we see Him, and see Him as the victor.

He prevails in chapter 5 to open the seals when all others have failed.

By His blood a countless multitude have been redeemed and translated, as seen in chapter 7.

His triumph at the end of all the judgments is announced in chapter 10.

He vindicates Himself and His two witnesses in chapter 11.

His name appears in the central verse of the book (12:10), in a passage which proclaims His lordship: "Now is come salvation, and strength, and the kingdom of our God, and the power of his Christ."

In the middle of the terrible chapter 13 He is the Lamb who has been slain to give life.

In chapter 14 He thrusts in His sickle and reaps the harvest of the earth.

In chapter 15 the redeemed sing their song of worship of the Lamb.

In chapter 19 He goes forth King of Kings, and Lord of Lords, and overthrows the beast and the false prophet.

And in chapter 20 He sets up His millennial kingdom and rules the world in righteousness. He then forever destroys the devil, and in chapter 21 makes all things new.

And in the last visions, chapters 21 and 22, we see Him the Lamb, the light, the husband, the temple, the life, the morning star, the Alpha, the Omega, the beginning, the end, the first, the last, the Lord Jesus Christ. When we classify these triumphs we see how Christ realizes:

1. The fruit of His cross.
2. The establishment of His kingdom.
3. The overthrow of His enemies.

He routs all evil; He reigns in righteousness; and He realizes all His purposes. The carpenter of Nazareth becomes the King of the world, and the crucified Jew becomes the Lord of the universe.

5
The Interpretation of the Apocalypse

5
The Interpretation of the Apocalypse

This is a thorny path, and one in which we must walk with delicate tread.

The whole subject of biblical interpretation is a formidable one, but nowhere more so than in the prophetic and apocalyptic parts of Scripture. Neither anywhere is there greater need for patient investigation and a tolerant and charitable attitude toward those views we do not accept.

No one mind, or system of interpretation, has a monopoly of truth, but all who are serious, devout, and studious have some contribution to make toward the more perfect understanding of the Word.

With this belief and in this spirit, I approach this difficult subject, and claim to do no more than indicate the possible lines of interpretation and say what at present is my own view.

The interpretation of the Apocalypse calls for the consideration of two things—the explanation and the application of that which is revealed.

Under the first we ask the question: is the language of the book literal or symbolical?

Under the second we ask: to what period or periods of time, and to what persons or systems do the things contained in it apply?

I. The Explanation of That Which Is Revealed

That is, is the language of the Apocalypse to be regarded as literal or symbolical? Some would say that it is literal throughout, and others that it is symbolical throughout; but surely the truth lies in a combination of these views.

There are certainly some things which must be taken literally, and others which must be taken symbolically. Nor is this a matter of opinion, but of fact, as can be shown.

There are many things in the book which may be either literal or figurative, and about which it will be well not to dogmatize; but this, at least, may be said concerning the whole, that the passages which are literal must be taken at their face value, and those which are symbolical are symbolical of something, and it should be our business to discover what that something is. In some instances we are told, and in others we have to search the Scriptures for their meaning. Generally speaking, it is a sound principle to regard that as literal which can be taken literally, and the rest as figurative. A writer on this subject has said:

"The mixture of the literal and the symbolic is so palpable and so frequent in prophetic Scripture that it seems quite needless to detain the reader by citations to prove it. He can scarce open a page in the prophecies without seeing examples."

Out of possible hundreds of illustrations we will give just three:

Psalm 22:18, 12, 13: "They part my garments among them, and cast lots upon my vesture." There can be no question about that being literal, for it was done at the cross.

"Many bulls have compassed me: strong bulls of Bashan have beset me round. They gaped upon me with their mouths, as a ravening and a roaring lion." There can be no doubt about that being figurative, for, of course, there were no bulls of Bashan at the cross, but fierce men who are likened to such.

Jeremiah 3:6: "Hast thou seen that which backsliding Israel hath done? she is gone up upon every high mountain, and under every green tree, and there hath played the harlot."

In this passage the mountains and trees are, of course, literal, but the harlotry is symbolical of Israel's idolatry, and is a figure of such throughout the Scriptures.

Psalm 80:8, 11: "Thou hast brought a vine out of Egypt. . . . [it] sent out her boughs unto the sea, and her branches unto the river."

There can be no reasonable doubt that Egypt means Egypt, that the sea means the Mediterranean, and that the river means the Euphrates. They are therefore all literal. But, of course, the vine is figurative, and refers to Israel.

Let this mixture of the literal and the symbolical be acknowledged as we read the Apocalypse, and, other things being equal, we shall be in a fair way of understanding its meaning.

We now give a few instances of things which we believe to be literal, symbolical, and doubtful in the Apocalypse.

A. Things Literal

1. *The seven churches* of chapters 2 and 3 are literal. They were assemblies of Christians in the time of John, at the seven places named, all in Asia. That they have a significance much wider than the then historical and local will not be seriously questioned, yet they were not imaginary, but literal churches.

2. *The personages* of the book—divine, angelic, and human—must be regarded literally. God, Christ, and the Spirit are not symbols, but persons. And so are the angels, the demons, and the devil. So also are the elders, the martyrs, the two witnesses, and all the redeemed Jews and Gentiles.

3. *War, famine, pestilence,* and *death,* as in chapter 6, must be taken literally, for these things could not symbolize anything but themselves, and their literalness is witnessed to by all history.

4. *The image* of chapter 13 must be interpreted literally. An image must be the image of something, and that something here is "the beast," who is, I believe, a person and not a system. It would be difficult to make an image of a system, but easy to make one of a man.

And the image cannot be a man, or assembly of men, for at least two reasons, namely:

(a) It would not then be an image;

(b) There would be no miracle in a living man or men speaking.

But that this image speaks is clearly regarded as a miracle.

This, therefore, is among the things which must be taken literally.

5. *Spheres and places* spoken of in the book must be read as literal; and of these there are many.

For example, heaven and the abyss are spheres, and not figures of moral states. Scripture has much to say about

a. *Heaven and the heavens*

Heaven was created by God (10:6), and is His "dwelling place" (1 Kings 8:30). Christ at His ascension entered into heaven (Acts 3:21; Heb. 9:12, 24), and from there He will come again (Phil. 3:20). The unfallen angels are in heaven (Matt. 18:10), and the reward of the saints is there (1 Peter 1:4).

This, and much more, proves beyond question that heaven is a place. The descriptions may be symbolical, but the thing described is literal.

b. *The Pit of the Abyss*

We read of this seven times in the Apocalypse (9:1, 2, 11; 11:7; 17:8; 20:1, 3), and it always refers to a place; from which, for instance, "the beast" emerges, and into which he goes again. As heaven is the sphere of the blessed, the abyss is the sphere of the cursed. It is a literal sphere of abode.

c. *Armageddon*

This expression simply means the place of Megiddo, a part of the great plain of Esdraelon. It is a real locality; the place where Deborah and Barak destoyed Sisera and his host; and where Josiah was overthrown by the king of Egypt (Judges 5:19; 2 Kings 23:29). What is predicted to happen there will literally happen there (Rev. 16:16). The word "Armageddon" is not therefore a name given to a great world campaign as is commonly imagined.

d. *The River Euphrates*

What can this mean but the river Euphrates (9:14; 16:12)? Surely if the "decline of the power of the Turks" had been meant (Guinness), there would have been some way of conveying that thought which would not have been positively misleading. I am disposed to believe that the Turkish Empire is in view in the judgments associated with this river, and that it is named to indicate the seat of that power. But the river is the river, and not the power.

e. *Jerusalem*

The study of this name in the Apocalypse is instructive as showing how we may distinguish between the literal and the figurative, for the name is used in both senses.

In 3:12; 21:2, 10, the use unquestionably is symbolical because we read this Jerusalem "comes down from God out of heaven," which the city in Palestine does not.

But in 11:2, 8; 20:9, the reference is certainly literal, and special care is taken to make this plain, for, although the city is also called Sodom and Egypt because of its moral character, yet we are not left to imagine that either of these places is indicated, the words being added, "where also the Lord was crucified."

This point settles several others in this chapter, especially the personality of the two witnesses, for what is said of them takes place in Jerusalem of Judea, and they cannot therefore be systems.

6. *Periods of time* in this book should, I think, be taken literally. I know this is a large question, and the interpretation of the whole book hinges on it. There are students of the prophetic Scriptures who work through the Apocalypse on the year-day theory, that is, that each day represents a year; and in support of the principle they cite Numbers 14:34; Ezekiel 4:5, 6; and Daniel 9:24. Thus, in one view, the time references are not interpreted literally, and in the other view they are.

That both these views cannot be correct is evident, and we must decide for ourselves, in the light of all the Scriptures, which is the right view.

The time references are as follows:

8:1—"about the space of half an hour."
9:5—"five months."
9:15—"an hour, and a day, and a month, and a year."
10:7—"the days of the voice of the seventh angel."
11:2—
13:5— } "forty and two months."
11:3—
12:6— } "a thousand two hundred and threescore days."
11:9, 11—"three days and an half."
12:6, 14—"a time, and times, and half a time."
17:12—
18:10, 17, 19— } "one hour."
18:8—"one day."
20:2, 3, 4, 6, 7—"a thousand years."

In the historical view of the Apocalypse:

The five months=150 years.

The hour, day, month, and year=396 years, 118 days.

The forty and two months The twelve hundred and sixty days The time, times, and half a time	=1260 years.

But there are some of this school who see how impossible it is to apply this year-day principle throughout with any consistency or reason, and who admit that in places the periods must be regarded as literal.

II. Literal Time Periods

One writes of 11:2: "What is meant by forty and two months? Literal time of 1260 days. This **must** be literal because of the angel having already sworn that there shall be **no more time or delay.** It is incredible that, **after this oath,** there should be 1260 **years** of persecution." (The bold face are the writer's.)

We, however, in these studies, interpret these time periods literally, reserving judgment on the meaning of the half-hour of 8:1, the hour of 17:12, and the day of 18:8, which may but signify periods of time without defining how long, though here, undoubtedly short.

It is not questioned that in Scripture some chronological figures are symbolical, but to assume that all figures in prophecy are such, is to introduce utter confusion.

That interpretation which is the simplest, the most obvious, and most harmonious in all its parts may safely be regarded as the right one.

We come now to the consideration of

III. Things Symbolical

Unquestionably a large part, if not the major part, of the Apocalypse is symbolical. Our difficulties begin when we endeavor to ascertain what is and what is not to be taken literally.

No definite rule for distinguishing between the literal and the figurative seems to be possible, except that the matter must be submitted to the decision of common sense, guided by all the circumstances of the case and any illustrative facts bearing thereon. There exists, I believe, an instinct of interpretation which may be cultivated by reverent and prayerful study of

Holy Scripture. I think such instinct may be defined as a delicate sense of the appropriate, and a natural shrinking from any interpretation which is grotesque, uncandid, or inadequate.

Of course, even on that carefully chosen ground judgments will differ widely, so that all one can hope to do is to offer the result of prayerful thought. Doubt, here, is better than dogmatism.

Yet we are not left altogether without guidance, for some things are declared to be figurative, others are interpreted in the text, and others become luminous in the light of other Scriptures.

A. Some Things Are Declared to Be Figurative

1. In 12:1, the "*Woman* arrayed with the sun, and the moon under her feet, and a crown of twelve stars upon her head," is called "a great sign."
2. In 12:3 we read, "there was seen another sign in heaven—*a great red dragon.*"
3. And in 15:1, "I saw another sign in heaven," *the seven last plagues*.

These things, therefore, are not literal, but figurative, and a careful study of them will take us a long way in the direction of understanding the principle of figurative language.

If the bowl judgments are revealed in symbolical language, we may naturally assume that the seal and trumpet judgments are also. And if this be granted, the back of the difficulty is broken.

Of course, as we have already said, there is here, as elsewhere, a close interweaving of what is figurative with what is not, and the most careful reading is necessary; nevertheless, it appears to me, from the clues given in the book itself, that the greater part of it is symbolical.

To the things declared to be figurative must be added those which are so obviously so, as to need no such declaration. Such, for instance, as:

4. *The tear-wiping* of 7:17. Meaning: the banishment of sorrow.
5. The *eagle* with the great voice of 8:13. Meaning: the swiftness of judgment. (See Deut. 28:49; 2 Sam. 1:23; Hosea 8:1; Hab. 1:8.)

6. *The little book* which John ate, found in 10:10. Meaning: knowledge agreeable and disagreeable. (See Jer. 31:33.)
7. *The sickles and reapings* of 14:16-20. Meaning: judgment and its instrument.
8. *The great chain* of 20:1. Meaning: means of restraint.
9. *The great white throne* of 20:11. Meaning: sovereignty, holiness, justice.
10. *The many books* of 20:12. Meaning: life-records of the people (?).

A most important and fruitful line of investigation is thus opened up.

B. Some Things Are Interpreted in the Text

We are told, for instance, that "the dragon" of chapter 12 is "that old serpent, called the Devil, and Satan" (v. 9), so we can be in no doubt as to his identity.

Again, in chapter 17, we read of a "great harlot that sitteth upon many waters" (v. 1). That, of course, is figurative, but who or what are the harlot and the waters, and the beast that carries her (v. 7), and its heads and horns? The angels who spoke with John have told us, so that there is no room for doubt.

> "The woman which thou sawest is that great city, which reigneth over the kings of the earth" (v. 18).

> "The waters which thou sawest . . . are peoples, and multitudes, and nations, and tongues" (v. 15).

> "The beast that thou sawest was, and is not; and shall ascend out of the bottomless pit, and go into perdition . . . that was, and is not, and yet is" (v. 8).

A comparison of verse 15 with verses 10-12 of this chapter, and with 13:1-10, must surely lead to the conclusion that this "beast" is not a world power but an individual, representing a world power no doubt, yet an individual, the eighth of the kings of verse 11.

> "The seven heads are seven mountains . . . and there are seven kings" (vv. 9, 10).

"And the ten horns that thou sawest are ten kings" (v. 12).

The importance of this chapter to interpretation is great, because the explanations given here are applicable to other chapters in the book.

This "beast," for instance, with the seven heads and ten horns, appears in chapter 13, and is frequently referred to elsewhere. That these are kings and not kingdoms seems certain, because we read in 17:12 that "the ten kings . . . have received no kingdom as yet," and the kingdom they do ultimately receive, they give to the "beast" (v. 17).

Verse 9 reads: "The seven heads are seven mountains. . . ." The "heads" and "mountains" are figurative, and one and the same thing, namely "seven kings." They cannot therefore be the seven mountains on which the city of Rome rested.

Here, then, we have interpreted for us by an angel some of the "mysteries" (v. 7) of the Apocalypse.

The woman (i.e., that great city, v. 18) sits on many waters (i.e., reigns over peoples, multitudes, nations, and tongues, v. 15), and is seen seated on a scarlet-colored beast (i.e., carried and supported by all the kings and all the members which make up the body of the beast).

Search for other inspired interpretations, as, for example, 9:1;19:8.

C. Some Things Become Luminous by Comparison With Other Scriptures

We have already seen that the Apocalypse is packed with the Old Testament from beginning to end. We therefore may expect much light upon it from that quarter. Nor are we disappointed. It is not contended that parallel passages in the Old Testament always have reference to the same things and events indicated by their use in the Apocalypse. But, probably, more often than not, they do refer to the same things.

The subject is a large one, and all we propose to do here is to illustrate it by selecting one item in each chapter which is lighted up by an Old Testament parallel.

1:7—**clouds**

By a comparison with Daniel 7:13 and Matthew 16:27, we

learn that these are not clouds of moisture, but of angels. Literal clouds would obscure Christ from the sight of men; but we read, "every eye shall see him."

2:17—**manna**

By a comparison with Exodus 16:32-34; Psalm 78:19, 24, 25; and John 6:48-51, we see that the manna given to Israel in the wilderness was typical of God coming down to men as life-giver and sustainer, and that Christ is the antitype. The over-comer shall one day in some specially precious sense, feed upon Him self-revealed.

3:12—**pillar**

Pillars in figurative language generally indicate strength and importance, as a reference to 1 Kings 7:21; Jeremiah 1:18; Galatians 2:9 will show.

4:6—**the living creatures**

It is impossible not to connect these "creatures" with those of Ezekiel 1:5-14. And if we compare further with Ezekiel 10:20, we learn that they are the "cherubim"; and that hint will take us back to Genesis 3:24.

5:5—**Lion and Root**

Genesis 49:9, 10 is the key to the first metaphor; and Isaiah 11:1, 10 to the second.

6:1-8—**colored horses**

A parallel passage will be found in Zechariah 6:1-8. In both cases they appear to be instruments of judgment.

"Black" (v. 5), for instance, denotes famine, as a reference to Lamentations 4:4-8; 5:10; Jeremiah 14:1, 2, will show.

7:9, 14, 15—**the redeemed**

The story of these redeemed Gentiles follows closely that of redeemed Israel. Both come out of great tribulation (v. 14 and Exod. 2:23; 12:41); both come under shelter of the blood (v. 14 and Exod. 12); both have a "tabernacle spread over them" (v. 15 and Exod. 40:2); and both commemorate these events (v. 9 and Lev. 23:40-43).

8:3—**the golden altar**

We have just read of the "tabernacle" (7:15), and now we hear of the golden altar, which stood, as we know, in the Holy Place, immediately in front of the veil which divided that place from the Holy of Holies.

We can see from this and other chapters how large a place is given in this book to the Old Testament institutions of tabernacle and temple. Indeed, the tabernacle and temple here seen in heaven are the substance of which the others were the shadow and type.

9—**the locusts**

A very interesting question emerges here. Are these literal locusts, or is the language figurative? The mind reverts at once to the prophecy of Joel.

There in chapter 1 we read of a terrible invasion of Israel by an army of locusts; and in chapter 2, if literal locusts are not described, the imagery is taken from a mighty locust swarm.

It seems to me beyond question that the literal locusts of chapter 1 prefigure in their four states or stages (v. 4) the four great Gentile powers of Daniel 2, 7, and 8—Babylon, Medo-Persia, Greece, and Rome.

And, it seems equally clear that the picture in chapter 2, whether of literal locusts or not, is descriptive of the past Assyrian invasion in the first place, and then of a desolating invasion of Israel by an army in the future. The point to be observed is that in neither case are the locusts themselves the judgment, but the types and precursors of judgment to be mediated through great armies and world powers.

There are those who contend that it is otherwise in Revelation 9, and that the locusts here are literal.

About this I have great doubt for a variety of reasons. As these locusts come up out of the abyss, it seems more natural to regard them as a demon army, and this view seems to be confirmed by the fact that "They have over them as king the angel of the abyss; his name in Hebrew is Abaddon, and in the Greek he hath the name Apollyon" (v. 11).

The locusts of Exodus 10 were, of course, literal, and were themselves the judgment, but that visitation was local and limited; the one in Revelation is universal.

As in this same chapter (v. 16) we read of a vast army from heaven (?). Is it not more than probable that the other army is from hell?

10:10, 11—**the little book**

The eating of this book has its counterpart in Ezekiel 2:9; 3:3. Ezekiel ate the roll of the book given to him, and in his mouth it was as sweet as honey. He describes the bitterness in verse 14, "I went in bitterness, in the heat of my spirit."

Eating is a Hebrew idiom for receiving knowledge, and the meaning in Revelation 10 surely is that the knowledge John received was sweet in the assurance that the prayers of the martyred saints would be answered; it was bitter in the solemn announcements of the judgments which were to form that answer.

11:4—**the two olive trees**

The mention of these takes us back to Zechariah 4:3, 11, 14, from which we learn that they represented two individuals, Zerubbabel and Joshua.

Therefore, in this passage also, they represent two individuals, and not two systems, as is often affirmed.

12:1—**sun, moon, and stars**

It might almost be said that if this chapter is understood the whole book will be plain. But misinterpretation here will blur the whole picture.

Will the Old Testament come to our help? There is only one Scripture in the whole Bible which corresponds to this one, and that is in Genesis 37:9, 10, where Jacob was the sun, his wives were the moon, and his twelve sons were the stars, and, altogether, they were Israel.

So in Revelation 12 it is most certainly true that the woman represents Israel, and the sun, moon, and stars the family of which the nation came.

13:2—**a leopard, a bear, a lion**

Go back to Daniel 7:3-6, and read of three beasts which were, respectively, like a lion, a bear, and a leopard. A comparison of this passage with the companion picture in Daniel 2 will show that:

The lion represents Babylon;
The bear represents Medo-Persia;
The leopard represents Greece.

Thus, we learn from the Old Testament Apocalypse that the characteristics of those three ancient empires are to be revived in the power of the latter end.

In this way Scripture illuminates Scripture.

14:17-20—**the vintage**

There are two passages in the Old Testament which not only offer a comparison to this section, but treat of the same event and throw much light upon it.

In Joel 3 we read, "Put ye in the sickle; for the harvest is ripe; come, get you down; for the press is full, the vats overflow; for their wickedness is great" (v. 13).

And we read with this Isaiah 63:1-6, where the treading of the winepress of the wrath of God is portrayed in vivid colors.

15:3—**the song of Moses**

The Song of the Lamb is given here (vv. 3, 4), but not the song of Moses; and, surely, for the obvious reason that the latter is given elsewhere? But where?

Some say in Exodus 15. Others say in Deuteronomy 32. It is enough for our present purpose to say that it must be one of these, and so the Old Testament again puts us in possession of the meaning of this statement.

16:12—**the drying of the Euphrates**

We have already said that we believe this to mean literally that the Euphrates will be dried so that a path may be made for the westward journey of the Eastern kings.

And the Old Testament confirms this. Not only do we have the instance of the Red Sea and the Jordan to show that such a thing can be done, but there are passages which declare that it shall be done.

In Isaiah 11:15 we read: "The Lord . . . with his mighty wind shall he shake his hand over the river (i.e., the Euphrates), and shall smite it in the seven streams, and make men go over dryshod."

In Isaiah 44:27 we read: "[He] saith to the deep, Be dry, and I will dry up thy rivers."

In Jeremiah 50:38, where the doom of Babylon in the East is announced, we read: "A drought is upon her waters; and they shall be dried up."

And in the same connection in Zechariah 10:10, 11, we read: "[He] shall smite the waves in the sea, and all the deeps of the river shall dry up; and the pride of Assyria shall be brought down."

A careful reading of these passages in their contexts should settle the meaning of the statement in Revelation 16:12.

17:12—**the ten horns**

A comparison with Daniel 2:42, 44, and 7:24, will show that these horns are kings, and that these Old Testament passages refer to the same set of events.

18—**Babylon**

There is great divergence of opinion about the meaning of "Babylon" in this and the previous chapter.

All that we will say about it at the moment is, assume it to be literal Babylon until it is proved that it is not. And read with this chapter Isaiah 13 and Jeremiah 50 and 51.

19:17, 18—**the supper of flesh**

A scene which illustrates this, but, it would seem, does not refer to the same event, will be found in Ezekiel 39:17-20. See also Jeremiah 12:9.

20:4-6—**the millennium**

Scores of passages in the Old Testament throw light upon this period. Reference might be made to Daniel 2:44, 45; 7:27; Jeremiah 3:17; 23:5; Zechariah 14:9; Isaiah 24:23; 9:7; Micah 4:7; Ezekiel 43:7. Tabulate other passages.

21:22-27—**the Holy City**

The imagery of this passage is taken from Isaiah 60

as a comparison of verses 23-25 in Revelation with verses 19, 20; 3:5, 16; and 11 in Isaiah will show.

This does not mean that the two chapters refer to the same time and state of things, but that the one illuminates the other.

22:2—**the river and the tree**

The first twelve verses of Ezekiel 47 will throw much light upon this passage, whose imagery is taken from it.

In Revelation 22:2, we read: "On this side of the river and on that was the tree of life, bearing twelve manner of fruits, yielding its fruits every month; and the leaves of the trees were for the healing of the nations."

And in Ezekiel 47:12, we read: "And by the river upon the bank thereof, on this side and on that side, shall grow all trees for meat, whose leaf shall not fade, neither shall the fruit thereof be consumed: it shall bring forth new fruit according to its months . . . and the fruit thereof shall be for meat, and the leaf thereof for medicine."

From these examples we see how an understanding of the symbolism of this book may be approached.

First, we must search out the things declared to be figurative.

Second, we must search out the things which are interpreted for us in the text.

Third, we must read the book in the light which all the Scriptures, and especially the Old Testament, throw upon it.

In this way, if we are diligent and candid, we shall certainly come to know much, if we may not know all.

One other matter requires a word:

IV. Things Doubtful

His courage is greater than his wisdom who finds no room for doubt on the interpretation of much in the Apocalypse. Equal scholarship and equal saintliness are found in opposite camps, and that should lead us all to be modest.

There are those who interpret the events of 6:12-14 literally; and there are those who take them to represent the disturbance of governmental powers, or the downfall of paganism.

Some regard Babylon of chapters 17 and 18 to represent

Rome papal and pagan, and some insist that literal Babylon is intended.

Some interpret the plagues of chapter 16 to be as literal as the plagues of Egypt. And some regard the language as symbolic.

Some have no doubt that the city described in chapter 21 is a literal city, and that those are its dimensions. Others are by no means so sure about it.

Much depends upon what one regards to be the interpretation of the book as a whole. If that can be settled, the parts will be interpreted in the light of the whole scheme. Let us respect the views of others while holding our own, and ever keep a mind open toward the light. In the study of this book, perhaps more than in the study of any other, we need common sense, a devout spirit, patience, and persistence.

6
The Application of That Which Is Revealed

6
The Application of That Which Is Revealed

In the interests of simplicity, we have divided the subject of the interpretation of this book into two parts—explanation and application.

The first is particular and the second is general.

Under the first we endeavor to know whether the book is to be taken literally or symbolically. Under the second we inquire to what period or periods of time, and to what persons or systems, the revelations of this book apply.

We shall have seen already, no doubt, that these questions are intimately related, and that the answer to the former question must depend largely upon the answer to the latter.

It is the latter inquiry we now approach.

There are four outstanding schools of apocalyptic interpretation:

1. The idealist—the book applies to all ages.
2. The praeterist—the book was fulfilled in the early ages of the church.
3. The historicist—the book is a history of the world, or church, or both, from the apostolic age to the end of time.
4. The futurist—the book speaks only of the last days, and so, yet awaits fulfillment.

Each of these positions is worthy of careful consideration, and each makes some contribution to the better understanding of the book.

I. The Idealist, or Age-long Spiritual Interpretation

A. This Interpretation Is Invaluable

In this view, the contents of the book are not statements of fact, but a "pictorial unfolding of great principles in constant conflict, though under various forms."

This interpretation is both arresting and attractive, and makes a powerful appeal to a certain type of mind. And undoubtedly there is a great truth here.

This book has spiritual values which lift it above all the controversy of the schools, and which make it, perhaps, the most encouraging and inspiring book in the Bible.

Of these spiritual values we may mention five:

(a) The graphic presentation of the age-long conflict between right and wrong, good and bad, heaven and hell, Christ and the devil.

This is an ever-present fact witnessed to, not only by the entire Bible and all history, but also by the individual conscience. This conflict has many phases, and is manifested in various forms, but it belongs to no one age or people. The principles of holiness and sin are irreconcilable, and are, therefore, ever in deadly antagonism. And these principles have their sources respectively in God and the devil, and their media of expression in angels fallen and unfallen, and in men regenerate and unregenerate.

(b) The issue of the conflict between the powers of darkness and light.

In this book no room is left for doubt as to that issue. The light conquers the darkness, the good overthrows the evil, Christ destroys the dragon.

The struggle is grim, and the suffering is terrible, but righteousness ultimately prevails.

That is a value which is independent of all schools of interpretation as such, and one which in these dark days we contemplate with grateful and joyful hearts. In this time of world unrest, when inevitably there is so much depression of spirit, there can be no better tonic than to be constantly reading the Book of the Revelation. Such a reading will lift us above the clouds, will carry us beyond the strife, and will transport us in vision to the time when "the war-drum throbs no longer, and the battle-flags are furled."

(c) The fact that this triumph is accomplished by and for Christ.

We have already seen that this book is all about Jesus.

He is the object of hell's hate and the object of heaven's worship. He is the invisible commander of the forces of judgment, and for Him, in the will of the Father, the issues are determined.

The dragon, the beast, and the false prophet are set over against the Father, the Christ, and the Spirit. The dragon and the false prophet work through and for the beast, and the Father and the Spirit work through and for the Christ, and it is the Christ and not the Beast who triumphs.

This consoling fact does not belong to any one view of the book, but must be and is recognized by all.

(d) The truth that the providence and government of God comprehend all subjects and events, and render them subservient to the best ends.

We cannot but be impressed with the comprehensiveness of this book in the matters of time and creature. It is shown that the spheres of heaven and earth and hell are all within the governmental power of the Almighty. And it is equally evident that past, present, and future are within the scope of His providence.

This is independent of any particular interpretation. God is supreme in His own universe, and, in a sense, inclusive and precise. He orders all things, in all time, in view of an ultimate purpose, known only to the Godhead, vast in scope, and unutterably blessed in its nature.

Read the Revelation with that thought in the mind.

(e) The intimate connection between the visible and the invisible worlds.

Throughout the Apocalypse, as in Jacob's vision, angels, to whom there are upwards of seventy references in the book, are seen ascending and descending upon that ladder, the ends of which touch earth and heaven.

And not only do angels tread these golden stairs, but the saints also by their prayers, which, offered on earth, are heard in heaven, and in God's good time abundantly answered.

This connection between the worlds, both in judgment and in mercy, is not true of any one age only, but of every age, and is the necessity not of any one set of circumstances and events, but of all.

We see, therefore, the great value of this view of the Revelation for consolation and inspiration, for the peace of our hearts and minds.

Further,

B. THIS INTERPRETATION IS INCLUSIVE

That is to say, it acknowledges and regards the measure of truth there is in all the other systems of interpretation, while following none of them.

The late Bishop Boyd Carpenter, an exponent of this view, says:

"It is hard to believe with the Praeterist that the counselling voice of prophecy should have spoken only of immediate dangers, and left the Church for fifteen centuries unwarned; or, with the Futurist to believe that eighteen centuries of the eventful history of the Church are passed over in silence, and that the whole weight of inspired warning was reserved for the few closing years of the dispensation. Nor, on the other hand, can we be thoroughly satisfied with the Historical school, however ably and learnedly represented. There is a certain nakedness about the interpretations often advocated by this school; the interpreter is too readily caught by external resemblances, and pays too little heed to inner spiritual and ethical principles."

Yet, "The visions of the Book do find counterparts in the occurrences of human history; they have had these, and they will yet have these, fulfillments; and these fulfillments belong neither wholly to the past, nor wholly to the future; the prophecies of God are written in a language which can be read by more than one generation.

"The Praeterist may, then, be right in finding early fulfillments, and the Futurist in expecting undeveloped ones, and the Historical interpreter is unquestionably right in looking for them along the whole line of history; for the words of God mean more than one man, or one school of thought can compass.

"There are depths of truth unexplored which sleep beneath the simplest sentences. Just as we are wont to say that history repeats itself, so the predictions of the Bible are not exhausted in one, or even in many, fulfillments.

"Each prophecy is a single key which unlocks many doors, and the grand and stately drama of the Apocalypse has been played out perchance in one age to be repeated in the next. Its majestic and mysterious teachings indicate the features of a struggle which, be the stage the human soul, with its fluctuations of doubt and fear, of hope and love—or the progress of kingdoms—or the destinies of the world, is the same struggle in all."

This is a powerful advocacy of that particular view of the Revelation, and it is as attractive as it is true.

Our parochialness of thought and circumscription of vision have robbed us of the things most majestic and glorious, and have resulted in a distorted view of the world and history.

> Our little systems have their day,
> They have their day and cease to be;
> They are but broken lights of Thee,
> And Thou, O Lord, art more than they.

We need to remember the truth of what Bacon says, that all divine prophecies "Have springing and germinant accomplishment through many ages."

And we need to remember that the scale of these fulfillments is very diverse, ranging from the individual to the world. The principles and forces in exercise in the conflict between good and evil are the same on every platform, whether of the individual soul, of the family, of the nation, or of the world; so that, whatever other interpretations may be claimed for in this book, this one holds good—that herein is a pictorial unfolding of the universal and age-long conflict, in an infinite variety of forms, between the principles of good and evil, with prospective announcements of the issue.

But while we adhere to the view just expressed, we believe, nevertheless, that

C. The Interpretation Is Inadequate

By inadequate we do not mean, of course, that it is lacking in breadth or depth, but that it extols what is general at the expense of what is specific.

There is no book in the Bible that is not capable of idealistic treatment; but, valuable as such treatment is, it must never be allowed to obscure the specific or deny the concrete in these writings.

That this is done by the idealist interpreters may be illustrated in the matter of chronology.

Bishop Carpenter says: "We are not to look for any indications of time in the visions of the Apocalypse; and what might have made this very plain is the employment of proportional numbers to denote the prophetic epochs in the Book. The anxiety respecting the 'times and seasons' has led many interpreters into voluminous errors, and has created a Thessalonian restlessness of spirit in many quarters."

And Professor Davidson says: "Most numbers in the Revelation should not be taken arithmetically, but indefinitely, because they are part of the poetic costume borrowed from the Old Testament."

Now, this is a matter of the utmost importance, and, in our judgment, the chronological data of this book are far from being "part of its poetic costume."

The idealist's view touches not only the Apocalypse but all the Scriptures, and, if true, is an interpretation of far-reaching consequences.

But there is in Scripture a "Divine system of times and seasons," a prophetic chronology, which, on whatever scale of time interpreted, must be regarded as arithmetic and not poetic.

Take, in illustration of this, Daniel 9:24-27, a key passage, the interpretation of which will settle the meaning of many references in other prophetic writings.

Here there is a "terminus a quo": "from the going forth of the commandment to restore and to build Jerusalem" (v. 25), and a "terminus as quem":

"until the consummation" (v. 27), the whole period being seventy sevens, or 490 years.

This period is divided into three unequal parts:

Seven sevens, or 49 years.

Sixty-two sevens, or 434 years.

One seven, or 7 years.

It is difficult to see how these figures can serve any end as "poetic costume." But all students of prophecy, so far as I know, take them to be literal; some holding that the years run consecutively; and some, that there is a long gap between the sixty-ninth and the seventieth "weeks."

In either view, one thing is clear, that the last seven years are divided into two equal parts, indicated by the words "in the midst of the week"; that is, there are two periods of three and a half years each.

When this point is reached it will be impossible not to connect these periods with the forty-two months, the 1,260 days, and the "time, times, and half a time" of the Apocalypse; and if this connection is valid the view of the idealist is not.

Therefore, we regard this system of interpretation as inadequate, not because of what it sees, so much as because of what it fails to see.

II. The Praeterist; or, Contemporary-Historical Interpretation

We must now consider briefly the Praeterist interpretation.

A. Statement of the View

It is so called from a word which means the past, and which views the book as having been fulfilled long ago. Chapter 1:19 is regarded as the basis of this system of interpretation. The book describes, says Dean Farrar, "the contemporary state of things in the Church and the world, and the events which were to follow in immediate sequence"; and outlines the victory of the church over the various obstacles which would have interfered with her progress.

Chapters 5–11 tell of the church's victory over the synagogue, or Judaism. Chapters 12–19 tell of her victory over pagan Rome. And chapters 20–22 tell of the felicity and glory of the church in consequence.

This is certainly an ingenious and suggestive conception, but must not be pressed as interpretation.

Those who take this view refer the larger part of the book to the Neronian persecution, and find in it a prediction of the return of Nero.

The seven kings of 17:10 are identified with the Emperors Augusta, Tiberius, Cadigula, Claudius, Nero, Galba, and Otho.

And the number of the "beast" 666 is found to correspond with the numerical value of the Hebrew letters in the words:

NERON CAESAR

N = 50   R = 200   V = 6   N = 50

K = 100   S = 60   R = 200

To the objection that, as the book was written in Greek, the value of those and not the Hebrew letters should be taken, is overcome by saying that with Jewish fellow-Christians the secret would be safe, but not with the Gentiles, who if they informed the authorities, would imperil the lives of all believers.

In order to hold this view of the book it is necessary to put back the generally accepted date of it more than twenty-five years.

B. History of the View

Dean Alford informs us that "this view found no favour, and was hardly so much as thought of in the times of primitive Christianity. Those who lived near the date of the Book itself had no idea that its groups of prophetic imagery were intended merely to describe things then passing, and to be in a few years completed."

The promulgation of this view "in anything like completeness" was by a Spanish Jesuit of Antwerp, named Alcasar, in the beginning of the seventeenth century (1614). He was followed throughout that century by some eminent expositors. Later this interpretation was revived in Germany, a large number of whose outstanding expositors have elaborated it. Nor is this to be wondered at, for the trend of German criticism has been to limit the views of the writers of Scripture to matters within their own horizon.

A few influential writers in England and America, also, have adopted this interpretation.

C. Criticism of the View

(1) We have already seen what a necessary and perfect relation the Apocalypse bears to the Bible and its separate parts, being their last fulfillment and consummation.

But if the Praeterist view is right, this book no longer bears that relation to all the Scriptures, for assuredly the consummation of the divine purposes was not reached in the fall of pagan Rome. The Bible would be singularly incomplete if it ended there; and the prophetic writings of the Old Testament would become most obscure.

As there is a fitness in Matthew's Gospel being placed first in the New Testament, though not the first book written, so there is a fitness in the Revelation coming last, even were it not last written; and the fitness is in that it gathers up and completes all that has gone before, and is the dome of the temple of truth, as Genesis is the foundation-stone.

For that reason, in part, we cannot accept the Praeterist view.

(2) But further. If, as this interpretation holds, the book was written of and for those days, and was presented in apocalyptic garb that its meaning might be open to the Jews and closed to the Gentiles; then it failed of its purpose, for it was not so understood by those generations. No doubt it ministered comfort to the people of God then, in their times of trial, as it has done to every succeeding generation, but beyond that, where it was accepted as canonical, its significance was looked upon as eschatological, and not contemporary.

(3) Yet again. If the Praeterist view is the right one, for an understanding of this book a liberal knowledge of the first three centuries of Christian and pagan history would be required, and that would take the book out of the hands of all who were not students of history.

This is a serious objection to any view which makes such a demand upon the readers of Scripture, whether of this or any other part.

(4) From another standpoint it may be, and has been, urged that surely the counselling voice of prophecy would not have spoken only of immediate dangers, left the church for sixteen centuries unwarned, and have left us in darkness as to what lies beyond.

Some may think that this objection destroys the force of the preceding one, but, in reality, it does not, for while careful students of history should be better able than others to see how God has been fulfilling His Word, yet, insofar as these Christian centuries are referred to in the book, the course of events is stated with sufficient fullness and clearness to require little or no outside knowledge for its understanding. We shall return to this point later on. Meanwhile, we hold that the Christian ages have a place in the Apocalypse, and that, consequently, the Praeterist view cannot be maintained.

(5) It might be yet further urged against this view that,

were it correct, only an antiquarian interest would attach to this book.

But, it may be said, this objection applies with equal force to many other books in the Bible. I think not. There is a prophetic element in all the Scriptures which keeps human interest and expectation sustained, and leads thought and affection on to a consummation which shall be the ultimate fullness of all minor fulfillments.

Surely we find no exception in the Apocalypse to that characteristic, but rather its grandest display.

For these reasons, therefore, which together constitute an insurmountable objection, we must reject the Praeterist interpretation of the Revelation.

7
The Historicist: or, Continuously Historical Interpretation

7
The Historicist: or, Continuously Historical Interpretation

This interpretation of the Apocalypse is the most difficult to present comprehensively in a short space, by reason of the scope of it, and the many important points which demand consideration. All, therefore, that is attempted here is to indicate fairly what this interpretation is, and to offer a few criticisms.

I. Standpoint of This Interpretation

This will best be set forth in the words of a modern exponent of it, Dr. Grattan Guinness. In his "Approaching End of the Age," he says it "is that historic Protestant view of these prophecies which considers them to predict the great events to happen in the world and in the Church, from St. John's time to the coming of the Lord; which sees in the Church of Rome, and in the Papacy, the fulfillment of the prophecies of Babylon and of the Beast, and which interprets the times of the Apocalypse on the year-day system."

Dr. Guinness argues that New Testament prophecy presents the closest analogy to Old Testament prophecy, and that, therefore, we may look for those wide outlines in the one that we find in the other.

"Now," he says, "the Apocalypse is the Book of the New Testament which answers to 'the prophets' of the Old." If, then, it contains predictions:

Of the first spread of Christianity,

Of the hosts of martyrs who sealed their testimony with their blood during the ten pagan persecutions,

Of the reception of Christianity by Constantine and the Roman Empire,

Of the gradual growth of corruption in the church,
Of the irruptions of the Goths and Vandals, and the breakup of the old Roman empire into ten kingdoms,
Of the rise and development of popery,
Of the rise and rapid conquests of Mohammedanism,
Of the long-continued and tremendous sufferings of the church under papal persecutions,
Of the fifty million martyrs slain by the Roman church,
Of the enormous political power attained by the popes,
Of their satanic craft and wickedness,
Of the Reformation,
Of the gradual decay of the papal system,
Of the extinction of the temporal power of the popes:
If it contains predictions of these events, which we know to have taken place in the history of the antitypical Israel, then we have a perfect analogy with the Old Testament.

In another part of his book Dr. Guinness enforces his belief with a very ingenious illustration. He says: "If in watching an exhibition of dissolving views we judge of the nearness of the conclusion, merely by the time that has elapsed since it began, we may have a vague impression that the end cannot be far off; but if we have held a program of the proceedings in our hand all the time, and have observed that each scene appeared as announced, and that only the final one remains, we have a certainty that the end must be close at hand, which is a very different state of mind."

And he proceeds: "A Divine program of the proceedings of this dispensation has been placed in our hands; they who avail themselves of it, they who study it, and watch the dissolving views presented on the stage of history, know how many of the pre-appointed configurations have appeared, melted away, and been replaced by others; they know the position on the program of the one now on the stage, and they know what remains! They lift up their heads, they know that their redemption draweth nigh—yea, very, very nigh."

This is certainly an attractive line of interpretation, and requires and deserves most careful consideration.

This view originated about the eleventh century, in the middle of that millennium of evil which we speak of as the Dark Middle Ages. "It was embraced with enthusiasm and held with intense conviction of its truth by the Waldenses, Wickliffites, Hussites, and Reformers." We are told that "It spread with a rapidity that was astonishing, so that ere long it was received as a self-evident and fundamental truth among Protestant churches everywhere.

"It nerved the Reformers of England, France, Germany, Switzerland, Denmark, and Sweden, and animated the martyrs of Italy and Spain; it decided the conscientious and timid adherents of the Papacy to cross the Rubicon, and separate from the so-called Catholic Church; and it has kept all the Reformed Churches since from attempting reunion with Rome.

"It was held and taught by 'a great number of outstanding men, among whom may be named' Luther, Zwingli, Melanchthon, Calvin, Sir Isaac Newton, Bishop Newton, Vitringa, Faber, Bengel, Birks, and Elliott.

"During the last seven centuries this system has been deepening its hold on the convictions of the Christian Church, and has been embraced by some of her wisest and best guides and teachers."

But, of course, the fact that this interpretation has been widely and influentially held, while significant, does not settle the question of interpretation. Our view of the book as a whole depends upon our application of its symbolisms. So consider the

II. Application of This Interpretation

A most important question at the outset is: Is this a Christian or a Jewish prophecy? That is, does it bear to the church, and to her fortunes in the world, the same relation that earlier prophecy bore to Israel, and to their fortunes in the world?

One can see at once how much depends upon the answer that is given to that question.

The historicist answers it most emphatically.

He says that the system that says: "Babylon means Babylon, and the literal ancient Babylon will, we are bound to believe, be revived," must be false.

"In the Apocalypse Babylon does not mean Babylon, nor Jerusalem Jerusalem, nor a Jew a Jew, nor the Temple the Temple; the system, therefore, that says 'all this Jewish imagery proves that the book has reference to the future of the

Jewish nation, and not to the future of the church,' must be false."

All this Jewish imagery is symbolic; these things are used as signs. Everything connected with Israel was typical of things connected with the church.

The things signified must, therefore, be Christian, otherwise the sign and the thing signified would be one and the same.

If everyone were as convinced as the writer Jews and their fortunes are scarcely glanced at in the book, which, starting from a period subsequent to the final destruction of Jerusalem and to the dispersion of the Jews, occupies itself entirely with the history of that church in which is neither Jew nor Gentile.

If everyone were convinced of this controversy over the main issue would be at an end. If the entire book is a prophetic program of the course of the Christian church from the Apostolic age to the Second Advent of our Lord, then, of course, its symbolism must be interpreted in the light of the history of the past 1,800 years. Babylon the Great will be the Church of Rome, and the beast, or Antichrist, will not be a person, but the final form of the Roman power. If those points of interpretation can be fixed the rest follows inevitably.

III. Points of Agreement

Objection to this school of interpretation has been taken on the ground that its commentators are hopelessly at variance with one another in their endeavor to harmonize the prophecy and the history. But it is only fair to point out that of twenty-six most distinguished writers from the Reformation to our own time there is remarkable agreement on the main points.

For example, they agree:

	Number Agreeing
(1) That trumpet six refers to the Turks	21
(2) That chapter 11 is the papal persecution of the saints	22
(3) That the beasts are aspects of the papacy	25
(4) That chapter 17 refers to Rome	26
(5) That chapter 18 is the papacy	26
(6) That a day is the symbol of a year	19
(7) That chapter 12 is the history of the true church during the papal ages	18

This agreement, to say the least, is striking. Other applications, about which there is no wide agreement, are as follows:

(1) The riders in the first four seals represent the Roman emperors of that period, and the horses the conditions then existing of prosperity followed by calamity.

(2) The fifth seal represents the era of Christian martyrs in the reign of Diocletian, about A.D. 300.

(3) The sixth seal tells of the politico-religious revolution under Constantine at the beginning of the fourth century, when Christianity became the State religion.

(4) The sealing of the 144,000, chapter 7, represents the spiritual revival among the saints which followed the revolution under Constantine, in which revival Augustine, the great expounder of the doctrine of justification by faith, was the leading figure. This doctrine represents the seal on the foreheads of believers.

(5) The trumpets of chapters 8 and 9 represent the decline and fall of the Roman Empire, from about the close of the fourth century to the middle of the fifteenth.

The first four trumpets tell of the destruction of the Western half of the Empire by the Goths, Vandals, and Huns.

The fifth and sixth tell of the destruction of the Eastern half by the Mohammedans and Turks, including the Turkish conquest of Constantinople.

(6) The "little book" of chapter 10 represents the period of the Protestant Reformation under Martin Luther in the sixteenth century, the book itself being the Bible, whose discovery by that noted monk was the immediate cause of that great event.

(7) The "seven thunders" are thought to represent the papal bulls of that period against Luther and his fellow reformers, and the sweet and bitter tastes referred to in the chapter, the joy of the reformers followed by the persecution subsequently felt as the result of their uncompromising testimony.

(8) Chapter 11 tells of the faithful churches, amid the general apostasy, from about the fourth to the sixteenth century.

(9) The woman and the dragon of chapter 12 represent the true church persecuted by pagan Rome.

The male child is the enlargement of the church at the time of

Constantine, and the wilderness flight of the woman points to the political decline of the true church under the increasing influence of the papacy.

(10) The Lamb on Mount Zion of chapter 14 represents the true church gathered around Christ, as over against the false church gathered around the Antichrist, while the new song represents the rejoicing at the Reformation.

IV. History's Movements

(11) The pouring out of the bowls represents events subsequent to the Reformation. The first five represent the French Revolution, and the terrors of the great European war, of which Napoleon was the chief figure.

The sixth bowl tells of the decay of the Turkish empire, and the preparation for the return of the Jews to Jerusalem, still future, but, presumably, rapidly advanced by World War I.

(12) The three unclean spirits represent the unholy principles of government, religion, and philosophy prevalent in these last days, and leading up to the final conflict between Satan and Christ at the end of the age.

(13) The judgment on the harlot (ch. 17) represents the destruction of the false church, that is, the papacy, yet future.

(14) The fall of Babylon (ch. 18) represents the destruction of the city of Rome itself, still future.

This summary of the view, taken substantially from Dr. James Gray's "Synthetic Bible Studies," gives a fair idea of the line adopted by the historicist interpreters.

It is laid down as settled that, as revelation is progressive, so interpretation must be, and that the Apocalypse could not have been understood at the time it was written, nor, indeed, for centuries afterward; and that only in the light of such events as the alliance of church and state under Constantine, the rise of the papacy, the Dark Middle Ages, the Protestant Reformation, and the French Revolution, is it possible that the book be understood. Thus, the prophecy was locked until it became history.

Dean Alford says that Mr. Elliott, one of the greatest exponents of this view, "Very naturally makes the great French Revolution a break, and the beginning of a new epoch in the history of Apocalyptic interpretation. From it, the continuous historical view seemed to derive details, and fix its dates with greater precision."

And, no doubt, World War I enabled them further to apply the closing chapter of the book.

If the historical view is correct, the structure of the book would be somewhat as follows:

1. Introduction (ch. 1).
2. The church in history (chs. 2 and 3).
3. Victory anticipated (chs. 4 and 5).
4. Great judgments (chs. 6 to 16).
5. Victory accomplished (chs. 17 to 19).
6. The church perfected (chs. 20 to 22:5).
7. Conclusion (ch. 22:6-21).

Having examined the standpoint of this idea, we must now offer a brief

V. Criticism of This Interpretation

It will, of course, be impossible within the limits of our present summary to deal with the many claims and detailed interpretations of the historicists, but several points of importance may well be considered here.

(1) First of all, we strongly deprecate the unwarrantable dogmatism too often displayed in the writings of this school.

An instance of this we see in the words already quoted: "In the Apocalypse, Babylon does not mean Babylon, nor Jerusalem Jerusalem, nor a Jew a Jew, nor the Temple the Temple; the system, therefore, that says 'that they do, must be false.'"

The same writer speaks of the connection between the history and the prophecy being "clear as daylight," a statement which, to say the least, is lacking in modesty, seeing that the most distinguished exponents of this school so hopelessly differ among themselves in this very matter.

For instance: Elliott interprets the sixth seal of Constantine, but Faber sees in it the French Revolution. Bengel sees in the star fallen from heaven (ch. 9) a good angel, but Elliott regards it to be Mohammed. Mede takes the locusts of chapter 9 which torment men for five months, to mean one hundred and fifty years of the dominion of the Saracens; but Vitringa says they mean the Goths and the Jesuits.

So long as there is such variance as that among those whose general view is the same, dogmatism should be avoided.

But such emphatic utterance is most uncharitable when we think of wholly different lines of interpretation from that of the historicists, for which there is an immense amount to be said, and which have been pursued by men of equal scholarship and saintliness.

I am aware that some of these latter have also spoken uncharitably, and such a spirit and attitude are not becoming in any of us. If a view is worth holding at all, it is surely worth holding courteously.

(2) In the next place, while not holding, for a variety of reasons, the view of the historicists, we recognize that there is a real value in it.

History repeats itself. All the angles of a pyramid are in harmony, so that we have a large pyramid at the base and a small one at the apex. It is certainly right to look for the fulfillment of the divine purposes all along the line of history; and, though I do not see with the historicists that their application of the Apocalypse is the true one, yet it is impossible not to see a wonderful general analogy in past history with what very many believe to be the yet future fulfillment of the Apocalypse.

(3) What was said about progressive interpretation is most important, and is widely held by those who do not accept the historicist view.

The historicist asks: "What should we expect the last revelation granted to John in Patmos to contain? Should we, judging by analogy, expect that, passing over in silence eighteen hundred years, crowded with events of deep interest, of stupendous importance to seventy or eighty generations of His saints, the Lord Jesus would reveal through this Christian apostle only the particulars of a brief closing crisis of earthly history, subsequent to the church's removal, and relating mainly to a future Jewish remnant?"

He answers: "Assuredly not! We should expect this final prophecy sent directly by Christ Himself to His church . . . to contain an outline of all that should befall that church, from the time then present until the Lord's return, with perhaps brief indications of subsequent events."

VI. A Question and Its Answer

We accept both the question and the answer.

The answer, because we believe this very thing is done in chapters 2 and 3 of the Apocalypse, and the question because we believe that that very thing is done in chapters 4 to 22 of the book. It is quite a mistake to think that if the continuous historical view of the Apocalypse is rejected, the book must be regarded as having nothing whatever to say about the church's history during the last eighteen hundred years. That is a false impression, as we shall see.

We believe in progressive interpretation, but we differ from the historicist in the application of it.

(4) The historicist affirms that the Apocalypse is Christian and not Jewish.

That is the crux of the whole matter. If that be true, controversy on the main issue is at an end. But is it true? We have strong reasons for believing that it is not. In the Apocalypse is presented the consummation, and in that we naturally look for a gathering up and perfecting of all the divine purposes previously revealed.

These purposes concern the world, Israel, and the church, and they are brought to view in this last book.

But there is a marvelous order and balance observable in the outworking of history.

God begins with the race; then He chooses Israel; upon their rejection of Christ, He calls out the church; when her history is complete, He resumes His dealings with Israel; and by means of them He comes in blessing to the whole race. When this is set out in diagrammatic form we see the wonderful plan:

(a)	(b)	(c)	(b)	(a)
RACE	ISRAEL	CHURCH	ISRAEL	RACE

Or, in another form:

(a) The Race (Gen. 1-11).
  (b) Israel (Gen. 11 to Acts).
    (c) The Church (Acts to Rev. 3).
  (b) Israel (Rev. 4 to end).
(a) The Race (Rev. 4 to end).

VII. What We See in the Book

If this is a true view of the course of history—and surely it is—then it is most natural that at the end the prominence should be given to Israel and the world, and not to the church. And this is what we see in the book.

We hold, then, that in the interpretation of the historicists the church is given far too large a place, and is seen where it really is not.

I cannot understand how it could commend itself to any thoughtful person—as apparently it has done—that the woman of chapter 12 was the church, and the man-child the extension of it!

It is equally difficult to believe that the Jews of chapter 7 are not Jews at all, seeing it says they are, and specifies the twelve tribes!

Some of the historicist arguments against these objections are very unsatisfactory and wholly inconclusive, especially their attempt to prove that the church is on earth at the time referred to.

Many students of both historicist and futurist schools believe that the bride of the Lamb is the church (ch. 21).

But there are many who do not take that view whose reading is entitled to some consideration, a consideration which it has not always received, as the following will show: "It is a painful and humiliating illustration of the length to which the desire to uphold a favorite theory will carry Christian men, that many futurists are to be found who actually do deny that the bride is the church, 'and even glory in their shame in so doing, as if this departure from one of the first principles of Christ' were an attainment of advanced truth."

We refrain from characterizing such an utterance as that, and can only hope that we may not be guilty of writing anything similar.

But that notwithstanding, I, for one, am not convinced that the bride is the church. She may be; but also she may not be.

To say the least, the historicist case is not proved.

VIII. God's Providence in the World

(5) In the historicist view, in order to an understanding of the Apocalypse, one must have a liberal knowledge of history. This is affirmed in their writings.

Dr. Guinness says: "A knowledge of history is needful to the intelligent comprehension of prophecy.

"Authentic history ought not to be deprecated as merely the wisdom of this world; it is something more, it is a record of God's providential government of the world.

"Besides, it is vain and foolish to deny that mental cultivation in general, an acquaintance with ancient languages and literature, with history and with a science are a help in the understanding of Scripture, and especially of prophetic Scripture.

"It is a strange estimate to form of the dignity of the Inspired Book of the all-wise God, that those ignorant of His works in nature and providence are as capable of understanding it as those familiar with them. . . . The ignorant Christian must be indebted to the learned in many ways."

I am one of the last to deprecate historical research and the largest accumulation of knowledge; and we gladly acknowledge that in hundreds of ways, and from many quarters light has been thrown on the inspired page by such knowledge, as witness the service of archaeology. But when it is claimed that in order to understand the Apocalypse one must have a liberal education, and be versed both in history and literature; or else be entirely dependent upon those who are, we emphatically dissent.

We believe that, while the course of history will shed much light on the sacred page, it can be understood without that light; that the Bible is a self-contained library, and that by "comparing spiritual things with spiritual" we may truly apprehend the meaning of the various books, the Apocalypse not excepted.

In our judgment this claim of the historicists can be used most powerfully against them.

Another point:

(6) If in chapters 2 and 3 we have an outline of the history of the church in this dispensation, then in chapter 4 the church is seen in heaven.

Her course run, our Lord has returned as He promised He would, and has taken her unto Himself; and she is seen there together with the saved of the Old Testament dispensation, before the throne.

If that be so, and the historicists grant it, for one of them has said, we "fully admit that the four-and-twenty elders and the cherubim of Revelation 4 and 5, include the church," then, it seems to me useless to attempt to prove that we can see the church on earth from chapter 4 onward.

Finally:

(7) On the year-day theory of the historicists, see how Daniel 9:24-27 would have to be read. If the half-week (v. 27) means 1,260 years and not days, then the whole period of which that is a part, that is, the seventy weeks would come to 176,400 years. But who is going to believe that?

And when we consider the futurist view, we see, yet further, that there are substantial reasons for rejecting the historicist interpretation, while recognizing in it remarkable shadows of the truth.

8
The Futurist: or, Eschatological Interpretation

8
The Futurist: or, Eschatological Interpretation

From what has been said in the preceding notes, it will already have been seen what view we take of the Apocalypse, and, therefore, it will not be necessary now to say much about the futurist line of interpretation of this book, as in the exposition of its various chapters we shall best gather its meaning and be able to judge its value.

I. The Substance of This Interpretation

Futurist interpreters, as the word indicates, regard the Apocalypse, in its major part, to be an unveiling of the things which are to happen in the last days, at the end of this age.

According to this system, the letters to the seven churches cover and predict seven actual and successive stages of church history. The visions beginning with the fourth chapter, and all the prophetical parts of the book, are to be viewed as a representation of events which are to take place shortly before the second advent of Christ to the earth, and the consummation of all things; the Israel spoken of here being the literal Israel—the "two witnesses" being two individuals; the days in the chronological periods, literal days—and the apocalyptical beast, under his last head, a personal infidel antichrist, who is to reign over the whole extent of the future Roman empire, and to persecute and triumph over the saints for just three years and a half, until Christ comes to destroy him.

In this view, the various visions—seals, trumpets, bowls—begin to be fulfilled, not at the time the Apostle John saw them, but at a point of time when the Jews shall have returned to their own land. These visions predict, in symbolic language, the state of affairs in "the last days"; the attitude of God toward it, and His activities against it.

That there shall be such an end to this age, the course of events throughout this dispensation seems clearly to indicate, and the analogies of history illustrate. The expulsion from Eden, the Flood, the confusion at Babel, the captivities, the Cross, and the destruction of Jerusalem in A.D. 70 are great notes in the history of failure; and yet another, and perhaps the harshest, is to be sounded before we can enter upon the harmonies of the Millennium.

II. The Soundness of This Interpretation

Chapter 1:19 has been quoted in proof of more than two conflicting theories. "Write the things which thou sawest, and the things which are, and the things which shall come to pass hereafter."

These, respectively, have been taken to refer to John's

(1) Gospel. (2) Epistles. (3) Apocalypse.

Others have used the words to prove that the entire book is future, no part of it having yet been fulfilled.

But the majority of futurists regard the verse to be a divine analysis of the book itself.

(1) The things seen—chapter 1: The Vision of Christ.
(2) The things which are—chapters 2 and 3: The Christian Church.
(3) The things to come—chapters 4 to 22: Post-Christian periods and events.

And this view receives confirmation in 4:1, where we read of "the things which must come to pass hereafter," corresponding exactly with the third expression in 1:19.

This interpretation does not require, as the historicists seem to imply, that the last eighteen hundred years of history are passed over unnoticed. They are not. It is only a question of the extent of the notice given to them. The historicists say it is in the whole book. The futurists say it is in chapters 2 and 3 only. In either view, this entire Christian dispensation is brought under review.

It is wholly a question of focus. The camera of the historicists is placed a long way back, and they see a distant picture with few details. But the camera of the futurists is brought up close, and they see a multiplicity of details in a very restricted area.

There seems to me to be unmistakable evidence in Scripture itself that this latter view is the true one. The only escape from it is by denying, as the idealists do, that there is any system of chronology in prophecy, or by denying, as the historicists do, the literalness of that chronology. But assume that there is such a system, and that the numbers are to be literally understood, and all will be clear.

We shall then see that the major part of the Apocalypse presents a near and detailed view of the last of Daniel's seventy sevens. The historicists deny that there are any "gaps" in prophetic chronology, and therefore make the 490 years of Daniel 9 to run consecutively. In this view, not only is their explanation of the 70th week forced and fanciful, but the 42 months, the 1,260 days, and the "time, times, and half a time" of the Apocalypse have nothing to do with it.

This latter we cannot believe. Scripture is not designed to confuse its readers but to instruct them; and the recurrence of these figures and expressions in two books of the same character surely must mean that the same period and events are referred to!

This we assume to be the case: that Revelation 6 to 19 is a minute unfolding of the 70th week of Daniel 9:27; and that, therefore, this entire Christian dispensation intervenes between the 69th and 70th weeks.

If this presumption can be shown to be false, the futurist theory will fall to the ground. But Dean Alford, who rejects this theory, frankly acknowledges the unsatisfactoriness of other interpretations of these chronological data. He says: "I have not pretended to offer any solution of these periods of time, so remarkably pervaded by the half of the mystic seven. I am quite unable, in common with all apocalyptic interpreters, to point out definitely any period in the history of the Church corresponding to the 1,260 days of chapter 12:6, or any in the history of this world's civic power which shall satisfy the 42 months of chapter 13:5. As far as I have seen, every such attempt hitherto made has been characterized by signal failure."

One further word, on

III. The Simplicity of This Interpretation

In this view, a liberal knowledge of profane history is not required in order to understand the Apocalypse, such a knowledge as the praeterist and historicist views demand; but only a thorough acquaintance with the Bible itself, in all its parts.

The belief that in chapters 2 and 3 we have a prophetic outline of the entire course of the church's history from the apostolic age to Christ's Second Advent, does not militate against this position, for, while a close knowledge of church history is of great value, it is not indispensable to an understanding of these chapters, for they are largely self-explanatory.

The seven progressive phases of the church's history will be found to characterize each stage of the story, and, indeed, all the churches are in each stage. By this means we are enabled to know what the whole course of the church has been and is to be, from what it is at the present time.

In conclusion let it be said that we have been greatly impressed with the fact that men of equal scholarship and saintliness have held interpretations of this book which have been and are regarded as contradictory and irreconcilable. This should have led both sides to speak with care of the view which they did not hold, and, also it should have led to the question, "Are these historicist and futurist views wholly irreconcilable?" The ways of God in history find many analogies in nature. In the latter we may observe slow processes of growth which come to sudden flowering. All the issue is in the process, and all the processes lead to the issues.

In like manner in history. History is not a series of unrelated events or movements, but is organic, every part displaying the presence and at work of great underlying principles. And is that not precisely what we find here? In Daniel 7:4-7 we read of four "beasts," three of which are named, and the fourth described. The three were "like a lion—a bear—a leopard"; and we know from Daniel 2 and 8 that these represent Babylonia, Medo-Persia, and Greece.

Now, in turning to Revelation 13:1, 2, we read: "I stood upon the sand of the sea, and saw a beast rise up out of the sea, having seven heads and ten horns, and upon his horns ten crowns, and upon his heads the name of blasphemy. And the beast which I saw was like unto a leopard, and his feet were as the feet of a bear, and his mouth as the mouth of a lion."

By comparing Daniel 7:7 with Revelation 13:1, we see that both these beasts have "ten horns," and from other passages we discover that these two descriptions are of the same thing. Yet, in this fourth and last are found all the characteristics of the other three, lion, bear, and leopard, a remarkable illustration of how "history repeats itself," and an equally remarkable illustration in history of the principle "slow processes and rapid issues." The historicists see the processes, and the futurists see the issues, but the former are wrong when they deny the issues, and the latter are wrong when they deny the processes. Without doubt, however much we may differ in matters of detail, the whole of this dispensation has been a preparation for its close; and without doubt, at the close, and within strict limits of time, all that has gone before will be reflected and consummated.

So we may say that in the Apocalypse we have prophetic anticipations and there we can be historicists, but certainly we have here also, prophetic revelations and there we must be futurists.

9
The Structure of the Book

9
The Structure of the Book

I. The Problem

What is the plan of this book? That is a question of the greatest importance to a right understanding of it, and one about which there is considerable divergence of opinion, according to the views which are held concerning its interpretation. It has been said (Erdman) that the book is made up of a Prologue and Epilogue, between which are seven divisions, each characterized by the number seven. Thus:

Prologue (1:1-8).
1. The Seven Churches (1:9–3:22).
2. The Seven Seals (4:1–8:1).
3. The Seven Trumpets (8:2–11:19).
4. The Seven Personages (12:1–14:20).
5. The Seven Bowls (15:1–16:21).
6. The Seven Dooms (17:1–19:10).
7. The Seven New Things (19:11–22:5).

Epilogue (22:6-21).

This sevenfold subdivision is easy to trace in all cases except Nos. 4, 6, 7, where it is more difficult to find, and is more doubtful.

The simplicity and suggestiveness of this outline will commend itself to all, and undoubtedly it is true. But here a most important question arises.

Are these visions presented in the order of fulfillment or of narration? That is, are they chronological and consecutive, thus:

Seals	Trumpets
1, 2, 3, 4, 5, 6, 7.	1, 2, 3, 4, 5, 6, 7.

Bowls
1, 2, 3, 4, 5, 6, 7.

that is, twenty-one consecutive judgments.

Or, are they contemporary, thus:

Seals.	1, 2, 3, 4, 5, 6, 7.
Trumpets.	1, 2, 3, 4, 5, 6, 7.
Bowls.	1, 2, 3, 4, 5, 6, 7.

that is, seven judgments described three times?

Or, do they partake of the character of both the former, each successive group of judgments overlapping the previous one, thus:

Seals,	1,	2,	3,	4,	5,	6,	7.		
Trumpets,		1,	2,	3,	4,	5,	6,	7.	
Bowls,			1,	2,	3,	4,	5,	6,	7.

that is, three movements or judgments, each doubling back on the previous one?

If this question can be answered it will not be difficult to discover the relation of the other parts of the book to these three distinct groups of judgments.

Let us glance again at the general contents of the book, which are as follows:

(1) The Son of man in the midst of the churches (ch. 1).
(2) The messages to the seven churches (chs. 2 and 3).
(3) The heavenly throne and those around it (ch. 4).
(4) The Lion-Lamb and the seals (ch. 5).
(5) The opening of the first six seals (ch. 6).
(6) The sealing of 144,000 Israelites (ch. 7:1-8).
(7) The Gentile host saved during the Tribulation (ch. 7:9-17).
(8) The opening of the seventh seal, and the sounding of six trumpets (chs. 8 and 9).
(9) The little book open and eaten (ch. 10).
(10) The two witnesses, their death and resurrection (ch. 11:1-14).
(11) The seventh trumpet, and jubilation in heaven (ch. 11:15-19).
(12) The woman, the man-child, and the dragon (ch. 12).
(13) The two beasts (ch. 13)

(14) The angels and their messages (ch. 14).
(15) The outpouring of the bowls (chs. 15 and 16).
(16) Babylon before and after its overthrow (chs. 17 and 18).
(17) The song of triumph in heaven (ch. 19:1-10).
(18) The coming and conquest of the King (chs. 19:11–20:3).
(19) The millennial reign and after (ch. 20:4-15).
(20) The New World and the New Jerusalem (chs. 21 and 22).

To those beginning to study the Revelation it may seem at first impossible to arrive at any intelligent and consistent interpretation of these various sections, but here, if anywhere, patience and persistence are necessary and are well rewarded.

II. The Clue

It seems to me that in 1:19 we have a direct intimation of what to expect as we take up this book to read.

"Write therefore the
Things which thou sawest;
Things which are;
Things which shall come to pass hereafter."

Attempts have been made to show that this verse will not bear the interpretation which many have put upon it, and which we are about to state; and, as we have already said, some have explained the words as referring to the Apostle John's writings.

The things seen—the Gospel.
The things which are—the Epistles.
The things to come—the Apocalypse.

But I am still persuaded that there is a meaning much more obvious, and that the verse is intended to be a summary analysis of the contents of the book.

In this view, the things seen will refer to the vision of 1:9-20—the Christ.

The things which are will include chapters 2 and 3—the churches.

The things to come will apply to the remainder of the book, chapters 4 to 22:5—the consummation.

And this is rendered surer by the fact that the last clause,

"Things which must come to pass hereafter" (meta tauta), is repeated at the beginning of chapter 4 where it is commonly recognized there is a new order of things presented.

Thus:

Chapter 1 refers to visions which John had seen—past.

Chapters 2 and 3 refer to what was to John, and is also to us still—present.

Chapters 4 to 22 refer to what was to John, and is also to us yet—future.

With this general idea in our minds, we must now carefully consider the matter of the book's structure.

III. The Plan

Those who accept the historicist interpretation of the Apocalypse must, of course, regard its various judgments as consecutive and continuous, and some who hold the futurist interpretation take that view, also. But among futurists the prevailing view, perhaps, is that which regards the various groups of judgments as doubling back over the period previously covered, entirely, or in part, with the purpose of filling in details.

For instance, Mr. Walter Scott thinks that 4:1–11:18, and 11:19–20:3, are parallel, the latter presenting details of the former.

But none of these views of the book's structure is quite satisfactory; so we must study its chapters again, noticing carefully each break in the narrative, and marking expressions that are repeated several times. By these means light may dawn.

We now proceed to indicate in a number of paragraphs what we believe to be the true structure of the book.

(1) We may certainly regard chapters 1 to 6 as consecutive. The first chapter is largely introductory. Chapters 2 and 3 outline the history of the Christian church.

We are then transported to heaven, and, in chapter 4, behold the throne of God and those who wait upon and before it.

God upon the throne (cf. 3:21) is about to pour out judgments upon the earth, but of created intelligences, none is able to initiate these as we see in chapter 5.

One, however, the Lion of the tribe of Judah, prevails to open the seals of the book of judgment. This He does according to chapter 6, where we read of the opening of six of the seven seals.

Up to this point all is clear and consecutive.

(2) But now there is a break. Instead of the seventh seal following immediately upon the sixth, as the first six follow one another, we have to go to 8:1 to read of its being opened.

(3) Nor are we to think that chapter 7 is under the sixth seal, for its opening words are, "After this." Moreover, the contents of this 7th chapter, in comparison with other passages in the book, make it impossible that it should be a continuation of the sixth seal judgment. But, let us proceed.

(4) In chapter 6, six seals are opened, and the judgment under each is carefully described. See verses 1, 2, 3, 4, 5, 6, 7, 8, 9-11, and 12-17.

But when we read in chapter 8 of the opening of the seventh seal, we observe that the judgment under it is not described. "And when he had opened the seventh seal, there followed a silence in heaven about the space of half-an-hour."

Thereupon we read of seven angels standing before God, to whom seven trumpets were given; and after three verses about the prayers of the persecuted saints, we read again of these seven angels and their trumpets, and become aware that we are passing into the second great group of judgments.

(5) But why is the seventh seal judgment not described? It is described much more elaborately than is commonly thought, for the seven trumpet judgments are the seventh seal visitation! But before they commence there is a pause.

(6) The trumpets, therefore, do not double back over all or some of the seals, but lie under the sixth seal, and proceed from it. For this reason it is equally incorrect to speak of the trumpets as following the seals. They do not follow, but are the seventh seal.

(7) From this point (8:6) we read on again, and the narrative is consecutive. Trumpets one to four are blown according to verses 7-12; then it is announced that the last three trumpets are to be "woes" (v. 13).

The first of these "woes," that is, the fifth trumpet, is sounded (9:1-11). Then it is announced that it is past, and that two more are to come (v. 12).

The second "woe" or sixth trumpet is blown (9:13-21), but before the announcement is made that it is past, and that another is to come (11:14), there is a long break in which most important details are brought to light (10–11:13). The contents of this long section indicate that it is not the sixth trumpet which is being described, any more than chapter 7 is a description of the sixth seal.

Is it not striking that after both the sixth seal and the sixth trumpet there should be a break in the narrative, and a long section inserted before the seventh of each is announced?

(8) In 11:15, the seventh trumpet is sounded; but notice that as the judgment of the seventh seal was not at once described (8:1, 2), but other matters brought to notice (8:3-5), so here, the seventh trumpet judgment is not at once described, but a revelation of exultation in heaven (11:15-19), followed by three chapters of particulars concerning the tribulation period, without which the other parts of the book could hardly have been understood (chs. 12–14).

(9) Bearing in mind that the judgment of the seventh trumpet has not yet been described, we pass on to chapter 15 where we read: "I saw . . . seven angels having seven plagues, the last, for in them is finished the wrath of God."

From chapter 16 we learn that these last plagues are the bowl judgments, the third great group in the book (chs. 15–16).

It must, therefore, be obvious that the bowl judgments belong to the seventh trumpet, just as the trumpet judgments belong to the seventh seal.

(10) Therefore the Bowls do not double back over the seal and trumpet judgments; neither is it correct to say that they follow the trumpet visitations. They do not follow because they are the seventh trumpet contents.

(11) And it is noteworthy that, as this is the last great group of judgments, they are all poured out in quick succession, and are all described, including the seventh (16:17-21).

(12) As we are expressly told in 15:1 that in these bowls "is finished the wrath of God," we need not expect another series of judgments, so that chapters 17–19:10 are added descriptions of what has already taken place.

Under the seventh bowl we read that Babylon falls (16:19); and it is that fall and its consequences which are described in

17–19:10, so that the story is not advanced by this long section.

(13) Then Christ comes to smite the nations, the beast, and the false prophet; and to put Satan under restraint for a thousand years (19:11–20:3).

And thus the Great Tribulation is ended, Christ is back on earth, the "times of the Gentiles" is brought to a close, for "the Stone" has fallen on the "feet," and all is in readiness for that period of blessing so frequently forecast in the Old Testament.

(14) In 20:4-15, the narrative is again advanced, for here we read of the millennial reign, the great conflict at its close, the final judgment, and the doom of the wicked. And beyond all this, the eternal state (21:1).

(15) Some expositors hold that 21:9–22:5 does not advance the narrative, but is an added description of the millennial state. But others believe that it belongs to eternity.

IV. Review

(16) Let us now review the ground already covered. Dropping out all explanatory matter, the order of reading, or the continuous narrarive, will be as follows:

(a) Chapters 1 to 3—the Son of man and the seven churches.

(b) Chapters 4 and 5—the throne of God and the sealed book.

(c) Chapter 6—the opening of six seals.

(d) Chapter 8:1, 2—the seventh seal announced.

(e) Chapters 8:6–9:21—six trumpets sounded under the seventh seal.

(f) Chapter 11:14, 15a—end of the sixth trumpet announced, and the seventh sounded.

(g) Chapter 15:1, 5-8—contents of the seventh trumpet announced, namely, seven bowls.

(h) Chapter 16 (15)—the seven bowl judgments poured out.

(i) Chapters 19:11–20:3—Christ comes and prepares to establish His millennial throne.

(j) Chapter 20:4-6—the millennial reign.

(k) Chapter 20:7-15—the ultimate doom of the wicked.

(l) Chapters 21–22:5—blissful eternity.

(17) We must now gather up the remaining passages and account for them. They are as follows:

(a) Chapter 7:1-8—the sealing of 144,000 Jews.

(b) Chapter 7:9-17—the Gentile multitude redeemed.

(c) Chapter 8:3-5—the prayers of the saints.

(d) Chapter 10—the little-book prophecy which John received.

(e) Chapter 11:1-13—the two witnesses, their death and resurrection, and the great earthquake.

(f) Chapter 11:15b-19—the Lamb victorious.

(g) Chapter 12—the woman, man-child, and dragon.

(h) Chapter 13—the two beasts.

(i) Chapter 14—the 144,000 and the six angels.

(j) Chapter 15:2-4—joyful songs in heaven.

(k) Chapter 16:15—announcement of Christ's advent.

(l) Chapters 17–19:10—the fall of Babylon and the jubilation it provokes in heaven.

(I do not now pronounce on chapters 21:9–22:5, whether it describes the eternal state, or is a doubling back to describe a millennial condition.)

These twelve passages fit into the other twelve, and are details which explain them.

(18) Attention must now be called to another important fact. After the seven seal judgments are announced (8:1), but before they are executed (8:7), their approach is intimated by "thunders and voices, and lightnings, and an earthquake" (8:5).

Again, after the seven trumpet judgments are announced (11:15), but before they are executed (v. 16), their approach is intimated by "lightnings, and voices, and thunders, and an earthquake, and great hail" (11:19).

These intimations are in the same place in each group of judgments, only the latter is more severe than the former.

(19) One more thing before we present the structure.

In chapter 10 a "strong angel" intimates that the last divine judgments are about to be executed; that there is to be "delay no longer" (v. 6); that when the seventh trumpet shall sound—the sixth has already sounded (9:13)—"then is finished the mystery of God" (v. 7).

Compare those utterances with 15:1, where we read of

"Seven angels having seven plagues, which are the last, for in them is finished the wrath of God."

From this comparison it is more than likely the subject of chapter 10 is "The Bowl Judgments" yet to be outpoured. The "seven thunders" of verses 4, 5 are, no doubt, those last judgments; and the "prophecy" of verse 11 must surely refer to what the apostle says in the remainder of the Apocalypse.

We are not left, therefore, to guess what was the content of that "little book." It was almost certainly chapters 15 to 19:10 of the Revelation, if not the whole section from chapter 11 to 19:10.

But for this view, chapter 10 would remain an enigma.

V. Outline

(20) Now we are in a position to present a general outline of the Apocalypse, which is as follows:

THE UNVEILING OF JESUS CHRIST

Prologue (1:1-8).

- A. Superscription (vv. 1-3).
- B. Salutation (vv. 4-8).

I. A Vision of Grace (1:9–3:22).

- A. The sovereign Christ (1:9-20).
- B. The seven churches (chs. 2–3).

II. A Vision of Government (4:1–19:10).

- A. The governors (chs. 4 and 5).
- B. The governed and the government (6–19:10).
    1. The seals (chs. 6–8:1).
    2. The trumpets (8:1–11:15).
    3. The bowls (11:15–19:10).

III. A Vision of Glory (19:11–22:5).

- A. The millennial reign (19:11-20).
- B. The eternal state (21–22:5).

Epilogue (22:6-21).

1. Words of comfort (vv. 6-17).
2. Words of caution (vv. 18-21).

From this outline it will be seen how symmetrical and closely knit are all the parts of this book; nor can we fail to observe the progress of its movements.

First *grace,* then *government,* and finally *glory;* and all focusing in Jesus Christ, who is the source of grace, the power of government, and the crown of glory.

"Blessed is he that readeth, and they that hear the words of this prophecy, and keep those things which are written therein; for the time is at hand."

10
Syllabus of Studies

Part A—Directive

Part B—Synthetic

Part C—Analytic

10
Syllabus of Studies

Part A—Directive
The Book to Be Read

Chapter 1

1. What five parties are mentioned in the opening verses?
2. How often in verses 1-3 does it say that this book is prophetic in character?
3. Who are here said to be "blessed"?
4. How many churches are referred to? Where were they? Name them.
5. In what verse or verses is the Trinity mentioned?
6. Where and in what connection does it say that we are "loved" and "loosed"?
7. Where was John when he received this revelation, and why was he there?
8. What did he hear and see?
9. In how many and in what particulars is the Son of man described?
10. What do the "stars" and the "candlesticks" signify?

Chapter 2

11. How many of the seven churches are addressed in this chapter, and which ones are they?
12. What three expressions are repeated in each of these letters?
13. For what is the Ephesian church praised, and for what is it blamed?
14. What are the Ephesians exhorted to do, and how are they warned?
15. Is the church at Smyrna blamed? If so, for what?
16. Who instigated the sufferings of the Smyrnian Christians, and how are they cheered?

17. For what is the church at Pergamum recommended, and for what is it censured?
18. What Old Testament characters are mentioned in the letter to Pergamum, and what is said of them?
19. With what sin is the church at Thyatira charged?
20. What things are promised to the overcomer in the fourth letter?

Chapter 3

21. Who are commended in the letter to Sardis? For what?
22. For what was the church of Sardis rebuked, and what was it exhorted to do?
23. Is there any connection between the conduct of the faithful and their reward?
24. For what is the church at Philadelphia blamed?
25. How often do the words "my God" occur, and with what are they associated?
26. Mark what is said in verses 7 and 8 about a door, a lock, and a key.
27. What do you understand by "the hour of trial" in verse 10?
28. What evidence is adduced that the Laodiceans were lukewarm, and what does Christ say He will do with them?
29. What is the remedy for their condition?
30. At what "door" is it that Christ stands and knocks?

Chapters 2 and 3

31. What features appear in each of the seven letters?
32. How often, and where are Satan, Jews, synagogue, works, and repent referred to?
33. How are the characteristics of the Son of man (1:13-16) applied to the respective churches?
34. At the close of each letter there is a promise and a command. Is the order of these uniform throughout?
35. Who gave utterance to these messages, and for whom was each one intended?

Chapter 4

36. Where is the scene of this chapter?

37. Who is He that sits upon "the throne," and how is He described?
38. How many other thrones were there, and who sat upon them?
39. What is said to be "before the throne"?
40. How are the "four living creatures" described, and who do you suppose they represent?
41. What is said to be the position of the living creatures in relation to the throne?
42. Where are the eyes of the living creatures said to be?
43. How many songs are there in this chapter, and in which verses are they recorded?
44. On what ground is the Lord God said to be worthy?
45. Is the Holy Spirit referred to in this chapter?

Chapter 5

46. Where was the sealed book?
47. What question did the strong angel ask?
48. From what spheres came there no response to the angel's inquiry?
49. What effect did this universal failure have on John?
50. Who spoke to John, and what did he say?
51. Who did John see standing in the midst of the throne, and how is He described?
52. What did the elders and creatures do when the Lamb took the book?
53. On what ground did they say the Lamb was worthy?
54. How many angels praised the worthiness of the Lamb?
55. Who sang the last song recorded in this chapter?

Chapter 6

56. Who called for the first four seal judgments?
57. What are the colors of the four horses, and what do the riders symbolize?
58. Verse 8. Where before in this book have we read of death and Hades, and what comfort does that passage afford?
59. Can you see any connection between these seal judgments and Matthew 24:1-14?
60. Who did John see "underneath the altar"?

61. What prayer is there in this chapter, and what answer was given to it?
62. What happenings attend the opening of the sixth seal?
63. What classes of persons are affected by the judgment under the sixth seal?
64. What prayer do they pray on whom this judgment falls?
65. Can you find in the next chapter an answer to the question in verse 17?

Chapter 7

66. How many angels are introduced in this chapter?
67. What were the four angels empowered to do?
68. From which direction did "another angel" come, north, south, east, or west, and what was his function?
69. How many were sealed, who were they, and how are they classified?
70. Who compose the "great multitude" of which we read here?
71. What is the song of this multitude?
72. Who sing the song of verse 12?
73. What do you understand by "the great tribulation"?
74. Is this multitude on earth or in heaven?
75. What popular anthem has this chapter given us?

Chapter 8

76. What happened immediately upon the opening of the seventh seal?
77. What scene is depicted in verses 3-5? And is there anything here which reminds you of the tabernacle?
78. Where is the judgment under the seventh seal described?
79. What is the proportion of judgment executed under these trumpets, and how often is it mentioned?
80. How are the last three judgments distinguished from the other four?

Chapter 9

81. How may you know that the "star" of verse 1 was a person?

82. Who do these locusts symbolize, and what were they sent to do?
83. Why do you suppose "five months" are mentioned?
84. What is it said men shall desire "in those days"?
85. How are these locusts described, and in what verse?
86. Who is their king, and what is his name?
87. In what connection is the river Euphrates named here?
88. How are the horses under the sixth trumpet described, and put down in figures the number of the horsemen?
89. Of what, in this chapter, is it said that men were guilty?
90. What proportion of men were judged, and what was the effect upon the remainder?

Chapter 10

91. In what previous chapter have we a parallel with the description of verses 1-3, and in what particulars?
92. Does this chapter tell us what the seven thunders said?
93. In what way did the angel solemnly swear that "there shall be delay no longer"?
94. When, does it say, the "mystery of God" would be "finished," and in what chapter is that event recorded?
95. Who took this "little book," and from whom? And who took a previous book, and from whom? And where in the Revelation do we read of other books?
96. What was John commanded to do with the book, and with what effect?
97. Where was the "strong angel" standing?
98. Who does the "they" of verse 11 refer to?
99. Verse 6. In what previous chapter is the creative power of God celebrated?
100. Where is the prediction of verse 11 fulfilled?

Chapter 11

101. What part of the temple was John not to measure, and why?
102. What city is to be trodden under, by whom, and for how long?
103. How are the "two witnesses" characterized, and for how long do they prophesy?

104. How are the witnesses protected from their enemies?
105. What powers have the witnesses, and do you remember any who exercised those powers before?
106. What happens to the witnesses, when, and through whom?
107. Where at last are the witnesses seen, and what happens to the guilty city?
108. What was said when the seventh angel sounded?
109. Read repeatedly the song of the elders.
110. Where is the temple of God located, what is seen there, and what happened when it was opened?

Chapter 12

111. How is the woman of this chapter described, and what was her condition?
112. How is the dragon described, and what power does he have?
113. Are the descriptions in verses 1-4 literal or figurative? Give proof.
114. From the description who is the "man-child" likely to be?
115. Who are the combatants in the war here spoken of, where is it waged, and what is the issue?
116. What does the "great voice" in heaven say?
117. Why are the heavens called upon to rejoice, and why is woe pronounced on earth and sea?
118. What are the fortunes of the woman after the dragon is cast into the earth?
119. With whom does the dragon go forth to make war?
120. What other names is the dragon given in this chapter?

Chapter 13

121. Who is it, according to verse 1, who stands upon the seashore?
122. How many "beasts" are there here, and where do they come from?
123. How is the first beast described?
124. From where did the first beast get his authority, and for how long?

125. How often do the words "was given" occur here, and in connection with whom?
126. What does the first beast receive from men which belongs to God only?
127. How is the second beast described, and how is he employed?
128. What was he empowered to do, and on whose behalf?
129. Who only were allowed to buy or sell?
130. Do you derive any comfort from verse 18?

Chapter 14

131. Where is the Lamb seen standing, and with whom, and how are the latter distinguished?
132. What was the voice from heaven like, and whose voice was it?
133. Who does it say the 144,000 are?
134. How many angels are referred to in this chapter, and in which verses?
135. What is the substance of the "everlasting gospel" of verse 6?
136. Where again in the Revelation do we read of Babylon (v. 8)?
137. What is to be the fate of those who worship the beast?
138. What is said about him who sits upon the white cloud, and who do you suppose he is?
139. How many sickles do we read of in this chapter, and who hold them?
140. What figure is used by which to describe the judgment of verses 17-20?

Chapter 15

141. What, in this chapter, is said to be "finished," and by what means?
142. Who are by the glassy sea, and how did they come there?
143. Where do we find "the song of Moses"? Read carefully the "song of the Lamb."
144. From where did "the seven angels" come out, and with what?
145. Mark: the "wrath," the "glory," and the "power of God."

Chapter 16

146. Summarize the bowl judgments in one word or two words each.
147. On whom does the first judgment fall?
148. Which of the judgments is preeminently retributive?
149. In which previous chapter did we read "they are worthy" (v. 6)? Compare this with that.
150. What was the effect upon men of the fourth and fifth judgments?
151. Look up on the map the river Euphrates (v. 12). What is to happen to it, and why?
152. What trinity of evil is named in this chapter, in what verse, and in what connection?
153. What great battle is announced here, when and where is it to take place, and who gather the kings together for it?
154. How many "great" things do we read of under the seventh bowl judgment?
155. What two cities do we read of under the last judgment, and what happens to them?

Chapter 17

156. From what is said here, is the woman of this chapter a person, a place, or a system, and of what is she guilty?
157. What other women have we read of in this book, and in what chapters?
158. Have we met in any previous chapter the beast of verse 3?
159. How, and in which verse does the angel interpret the beast, and what is said to be his origin and destiny?
160. Who will wonder after the beast, and why?
161. How are the seven heads and the ten horns explained?
162. Who shall make war against the Lamb, with what result, and how is the result accounted for?
163. How are the waters of verse 1 interpreted?
164. What is to be the fate of this "mother of harlots"?
165. Who are they that hate and destroy the harlot, and who led them to do so?

Chapter 18

166. Where again in this book are found the words of verse 2?
167. How is the fate of Babylon described, and what is the reason given?
168. Who are bidden come out of Babylon, and for what reason, and who is the speaker?
169. In which verses is recorded the entire reversal of Babylon's fortunes?
170. How do the kings of the earth regard Babylon's overthrow, and what do they say?
171. What other classes of persons lament the overthrow, and for what reasons?
172. How many kinds of merchandise are specified in verses 11-13?
173. What two sentences are each repeated three times in this chapter, and in which verses? What other expression occurs six times?
174. Who was bidden rejoice over the fall of Babylon?
175. How is that fall symbolized, and by whom?

Chapter 19

176. What are the occasions of the joy in heaven described in verses 1-10?
177. What woman do we read of in this chapter? Contrast her with the woman of chapter 17.
178. What suppers do we read of here, and in which verses?
179. How many hallelujahs are recorded here, and who utter them?
180. What is it said fine linen symbolizes?
181. Where before have we read of "a white horse" (v. 11)? Compare the riders.
182. What titles are given to Christ in this chapter?
183. Who accompany the rider on the white horse, and for what purpose?
184. How is Christ described in verses 11-16? Compare the passage with the description in chapter 1.
185. Where before have we read of "a rod of iron," and in what connection?
186. Of what previous passage does verse 18 remind you?

187. Who oppose Christ in this great conflict, and what is their fate?
188. Who is the Lamb's wife, and who are the guests (vv. 7, 9)?
189. In what great oratorio do the closing words of verse 16 occur?
190. Which chapter is devoted to the beast and the false prophet of verse 20?

Chapter 20

191. What is done with Satan, by whom, and for how long?
192. Who are they who reign with Christ during the Millennium?
193. What does this chapter teach about the first resurrection?
194. How are the nations affected by Satan's power, and in which verse is his influence defined?
195. What will be the effect of the loosing of Satan?
196. What city is the focus of the last war?
197. Where is Satan put at the beginning of the Millennium, and where after?
198. What witness does this chapter bear to eternal torment?
199. Who are judged at the great white throne, and what is the criterion?
200. Mark well what this chapter says about "the lake of fire."

Chapter 21

201. What "new" things do we read of here?
202. What familiar things are finally to be done away?
203. What is promised to the overcomer, and who are to suffer "the second death"?
204. Where before have we read of the wife of the Lamb (v. 9), and who is she?
205. How many gates has the Holy City, and what are written on them?
206. What is the shape of the city, and whose names are on the foundations?
207. Why is there no temple in it?
208. How is the city lighted?
209. What is the relation of the nations to the city?
210. Who are excluded from the city?

Chapter 22

211. What features of Genesis 1 to 3 reappear here?
212. What things, are we told, are to be no more?
213. In which verses does it say that the servants are also kings?
214. Where before, and in what connection, do we get the expression "for ever and ever"?
215. Who are here pronounced "blessed," and where have we read of them before?
216. Who showed John all these things?
217. How often is the Second Advent referred to here?
218. How is Jesus described in this chapter?
219. Who are invited to "come" in verse 17?
220. Consider the solemn warning given with respect to this book (vv. 18, 19).

General

221. How often does the word "seven" occur in the Revelation? Enumerate the things of which there are seven.
222. What do "Alpha" and "Omega" mean? Who are called by these names, and where?
223. Draw a map in outline of Asia Minor showing its relation to Italy and Palestine, and put in the places addressed in chapters 2 and 3.
224. Approximately, how many Old Testament quotations are there in the Revelation? How many references to the Old Testament?
225. What things in this book are declared to be "signs" or "wonders"?
226. What tribes are omitted from the list in chapter 7, and why, do you suppose?
227. How many references to angels are there in this book, and how does this impress you?
228. How many references are there to the devil, by what names, and in what connections?
229. Where in Daniel are the three beasts of 13:2 mentioned, and are the passages related?
230. What references are there to the temple, and where?
231. How is heaven described in this book?
232. To whom are the invitations of 22:17 addressed?

Part B—Synthetic
The Book As a Whole

I. The Human Author of the Book

THE CONTROVERSY
THE CONCLUSION

A. The home and occupation of John
B. The discipleship and service-life of John
C. The references to John in the history of the church
D. The portrait of John derived from tradition
E. The place of John in the apostolic age
F. The character of John as reflected in his writings

II. The Relations of the Book

A. To the whole Bible
B. To the Old Testament
C. To the New Testament
D. To the Book of Daniel
E. To the Book of Genesis

III. The Place of the Book in the Prophetic Program

THE SEVENTY WEEKS OF DANIEL (9:22-27)

A. The sixty-nine weeks
B. The interval
C. The seventieth week

IV. The Chapter Contents of the Book

1. Alpha
2, 3. Churches
4. Thrones
5. Lion-Lamb
6. Seals
7. Multitude
8. Trumpets
9. Locusts
10. Little Book
11. Witnesses
12. Dragon
13. Beasts
14. Angels
15. Wrath
16. Bowls
17. Woman
18. Babylon
19. Suppers
20. Millennium
21. Holy City
22. Advent

V. The Central Subject of the Book—Christ

THE UNVEILINGS OF CHRIST

A. The personal unveiling
B. The official unveiling
C. The dispensational unveiling

THE UTTERANCES OF CHRIST

A. The passages
B. The teaching
C. The standpoint

THE RELATIONS OF CHRIST

A. To heaven
B. To earth
C. To hell

THE ACTIVITIES OF CHRIST

A. In relation to the church
B. In relation to Israel
C. In relation to the world

THE TRIUMPHS OF CHRIST

A. The fruit of His cross
B. The overthrow of His enemies
C. The establishment of His kingdom

VI. The Interpretation of the Book

THE EXPLANATION OF THE THINGS REVEALED

A. Things literal
B. Things symbolical
C. Things doubtful

THE APPLICATION OF THE THINGS REVEALED

A. The Idealist,
or, Age-long Spiritual Interpretation
1. This interpretation is invaluable
2. This interpretation is inclusive
3. This interpretation is inadequate

B. The Praeterist,
or, Contemporary-Historical Interpretation
1. Statement of the view

2. History of the view
3. Rejection of the view

C. The Historicist, or, Continuously Historical Interpretation
1. Standpoint of this interpretation
2. Application of this interpretation
3. Criticism of this interpretation

D. The Futurist, or, Eschatological Interpretation
1. The substance of it
2. The soundness of it
3. The simplicity of it

VII. The Structure of the Book

A. The problem
B. The clue
C. The plan

Part C—Analytic
The Book in Its Parts

The Plan of the Revelation

The Prologue (1:1-8)
Superscription (vv. 1-3)
Salutation (vv. 4-8)

I. A Vision of Grace (1:9–3:22)

A. The Sovereign Christ (1:9-20)
B. The Seven Churches (chs. 2–3)

II. A Vision of Government (4–19:10)

A. The Governors (chs. 4–5)
B. The Government (chs. 6–19:10)
   1. The Seal Judgments (6–8:1)
   2. The Trumpet Judgments (8:2–11:13)
   3. The Bowl Judgments (11:14–19:10)

III. A Vision of Glory (19:11–22:5)

A. The Millennial Reign (19:11–20)
B. The Eternal State (21–22:5)

The Epilogue (22:6-21)
Words of comfort (vv. 6-17)
Words of caution (vv. 18-21)

I. The Prologue (1:1-8)

A. The Superscription (vv. 1-3)
   1. The date of the book
   2. The title
   3. The subject
   4. The character
   5. The communication
   6. The value
B. The Salutation (vv. 4-8)
   1. The writer
   2. The readers
   3. The greeting
   4. The ascription of praise

5. The prophetic announcement
6. The divine verification

II. A Vision of Grace (1:9–3:22)

A. The Sovereign Christ (1:9-20)
   1. Occasion of the Vision (vv. 9-11)
      a. The physical circumstances
      b. The spiritual circumstances
   2. Object of the Vision (vv. 12-16)
      a. Its setting, verse 12: The churches
      b. Its Substance, verses 13-16: The Christ
   3. Outcome of the Vision (vv. 17-20)
      a. The apostle comforted (vv. 17, 18)
      b. The apostle commanded (vv. 19, 20)

B. The Seven Churches (chs. 2–3)
   1. The Churches
      a. Their number
      b. Their order
      c. Their import
   2. The Letters
      a. Their significance
      b. Their characteristics
      c. Their message

III. A Vision of Government (4:1–19:10)

The Governors (chs. 4–5)

A. The Almighty (ch. 4)

B. The Lion-Lamb (ch. 5)
   1. The Heavenly Throne
      a. Setting of the vision
      b. Scene of the vision
      c. Significance of the vision
   2. The Heavenly Throng
      a. The elders
      b. The zoa
      c. The angels
   3. The Heavenly Theme
      a. The trisagion song
      b. The creation song
      c. The redemption song

The Government (6–19:10)

A. The Preparation for Judgment (chs. 4–5)
   1. The vision of the sealed book
   2. The opening of the sealed book
   3. The subject of the sealed book
B. The Execution of Judgment (6–19:10)
   Preliminary considerations:
   1. The purpose of these judgments
   2. The period of these judgments
   3. The plan of these judgments
C. The Seal Judgments (6–8:5)
   1. Four Seals (6:1-8)
      a. The First Seal (vv. 1, 2)
         1) The white horse
         2) The rider with the bow
      b. The Second Seal (vv. 3, 4)
         1) The red horse
         2) The rider with the sword
      c. The Third Seal (vv. 5, 6)
         1) The black horse
         2) The rider with the balance
      d. The Fourth Seal (vv. 7, 8)
         1) The pale horse
         2) The rider with Hades
   2. Three Seals (6:9–8:5)
      a. The Fifth Seal (6:9-11)
         1) The souls under the altar
         2) Their cry and the reply
      b. The Sixth Seal (6:12-17)
         1) The great convulsion
         2) Effects in heaven and earth
            (Parenthesis No. 1. Chapter 7)
            a) The Sealed Jewish Remnant (vv. 1-8)
            b) The Saved Gentile Multitude (vv. 9-17)
      c. The Seventh Seal (8:1-5)
         1) The angels with the trumpets
         2) The angel with the censer
D. The Trumpet Judgments (8:6–14)
   1. Four Trumpets (8:6-12)
      The seven announced (v. 6)

a. The First Trumpet (v. 7)
   1) The earth smitten
   2) Third part burnt up
b. The Second Trumpet (vv. 8, 9)
   1) The sea smitten
   2) Third part became blood
c. The Third Trumpet (vv. 10, 11)
   1) The waters smitten
   2) Third part made bitter
d. The Fourth Trumpet (v. 12 [13])
   1) The heavens smitten
   2) Third part darkened

2. Three Trumpets (8:13–14)
   The last three announced (8:13)
   a. The Fifth Trumpet (9:1-12)
      1) The star and the locusts
      2) The hurt of men
   b. The Sixth Trumpet (9:13-21)
      1) The heavenly horsemen
      2) The death of men
         (Parenthesis No. 2. Chapters 10–11:14)
         a) The Little Book (ch. 10)
         b) The Two Witnesses (11:1-4)
   c. The Seventh Trumpet (9:15-19)
      1) The sounding of the trumpet
      2) The opening of the temple
         (Parenthesis No. 3. Chapters 12–14)
         a) The Woman and the Dragon (ch. 12)
         b) The Two Beasts (ch. 13)
         c) The Lamb and the 144,000 (14:1-5)
         d) The Angels and the Son (14:6-20)

E. The Bowl Judgments (15–19:10)
   1. Preparation for the Judgments (ch. 15)
      a. The Sign of the Angels with the Plagues (v. 1)
         (Parenthesis No. 4. Chapter 15:2-4)
         The Songs of the Overcomers
      b. The Emergence of the Angels From the Temple (vv. 5-8)
   2. Execution of the Judgments (16–19:10)
      The angels commissioned (16:1)

a. The First Bowl (vv. 1, 2)
   1) Into the earth
   2) Grievous sores
b. The Second Bowl (v. 3)
   1) Into the sea
   2) Blood and death
c. The Third Bowl (vv. 4-7)
   1) Into the rivers
   2) Waters of blood
d. The Fourth Bowl (vv. 8, 9)
   1) Upon the sun
   2) Men scorched with fire
e. The Fifth Bowl (vv. 10, 11)
   1) Upon the throne of the beast
   2) His kingdom darkened
f. The Sixth Bowl (vv. 12-16)
   1) Upon the great river
   2) The Euphrates dried up
      (Parenthesis No. 5. Chapter 16:13-16)
      a) Three Demons Like Frogs (vv. 13, 14, 16)
      b) The Second Advent Announced (v. 15)
g. The Seventh Bowl (vv. 17-21)
   1) Upon the air
   2) Widespread destruction
      (Parenthesis No. 6. Chapters 17–19:10)
      a) The Harlot and the Beast (17–19:4)
         Babylon *morally* (ch. 17)
            A Woman. The Principle.
         Babylon *physically* (18–19:4)
            A City. The Place.
      b) The Bride and the Lamb (19:5-10)
         (1) The song
         (2) The supper

IV. A Vision of Glory (19:11–22:5)

A. The Millennial Reign (19:11–20)
   1. Before it (19:11–20:3)
      a. The King comes to battle (19:11-16)
      b. The issue of the conflict (19:17-21)
      c. The binding of the devil (20:1-3)

2. During it (20:4-6)
   a. The Messiah and His saints (v. 4)
   b. The unregenerate dead (v. 5)
   c. The first resurrection (v. 6)
3. After it (20:7-15)
   a. The last revolt (vv. 7-9)
   b. The devil's doom (v. 10)
   c. The great white throne (vv. 11-15)

B. The Eternal State (21–22:5)
   1. The descent of the city (21:1-8)
   2. The description of the city (21:9-21)
   3. The delights of the city (21:22–22:5)

C. The Epilogue (22:6-21)
   1. Words of comfort (vv. 6-17)
   2. Words of caution (vv. 18-21)

THE REVELATION: A PLAN OF THE BOOK.

PROLOGUE (1:1-8)

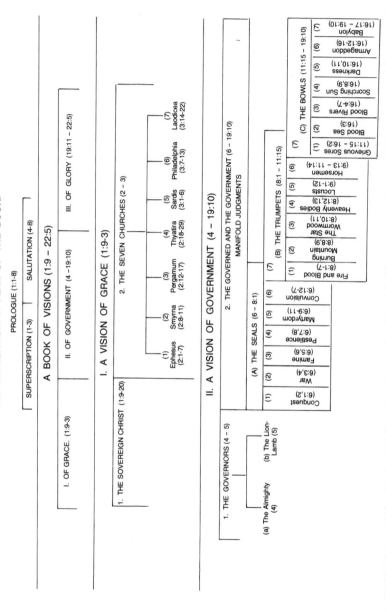

- SUPERSCRIPTION (1-3)
- SALUTATION (4-8)

A BOOK OF VISIONS (1:9 – 22:5)

- I. OF GRACE. (1:9-3)
- II. OF GOVERNMENT (4 –19:10)
- III. OF GLORY (19:11 – 22:5)

I. A VISION OF GRACE (1:9-3)

1. THE SOVEREIGN CHRIST (1:9-20)
2. THE SEVEN CHURCHES (2 – 3)
   - (1) Ephesus (2:1-7)
   - (2) Smyrna (2:8-11)
   - (3) Pergamum (2:12-17)
   - (4) Thyatira (2:18-29)
   - (5) Sardis (3:1-6)
   - (6) Philadelphia (3:7-13)
   - (7) Laodicea (3:14-22)

II. A VISION OF GOVERNMENT (4 – 19:10)

1. THE GOVERNORS (4 – 5)
   - (a) The Almighty (4)
   - (b) The Lion-Lamb (5)
2. THE GOVERNED AND THE GOVERNMENT (6 – 19:10)
   MANIFOLD JUDGMENTS
   - (A) THE SEALS (6 – 8:1)
     - (1) Conquest (6:1,2)
     - (2) War (6:3,4)
     - (3) Famine (6:5,6)
     - (4) Pestilence (6:7,8)
     - (5) Martyrdom (6:9-11)
     - (6) Convulsion (6:12-7)
     - (7) (B) THE TRUMPETS (8:1 – 11:15)
       - (1) Fire and Blood (8:1-7)
       - (2) Burning Mountain (8:8,9)
       - (3) The Star Wormwood (8:10,11)
       - (4) Heavenly Bodies (8:12,13)
       - (5) Locusts (9:1-12)
       - (6) Horsemen (9:13 – 11:14)
       - (7) (C) THE BOWLS (11:15 – 19:10)
         - (1) Grievous Sores (11:15 - 16:2)
         - (2) Blood Sea (16:3)
         - (3) Blood Rivers (16:4-7)
         - (4) Scorching Sun (16:8,9)
         - (5) Darkness (16:10,11)
         - (6) Armageddon (16:12-16)
         - (7) Babylon (16:17 – 19:10)

EXPLANATORY PASSAGES IN THE VISION OF GOVERNMENT

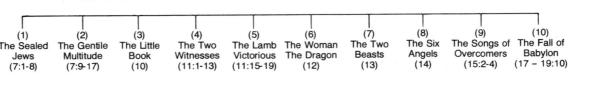

- (1) The Sealed Jews (7:1-8)
- (2) The Gentile Multitude (7:9-17)
- (3) The Little Book (10)
- (4) The Two Witnesses (11:1-13)
- (5) The Lamb Victorious (11:15-19)
- (6) The Woman The Dragon (12)
- (7) The Two Beasts (13)
- (8) The Six Angels (14)
- (9) The Songs of Overcomers (15:2-4)
- (10) The Fall of Babylon (17 – 19:10)

III. A VISION OF GLORY (19:11 – 22:5)

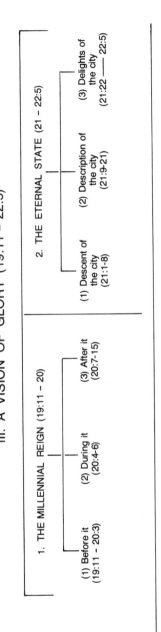

1. THE MILLENNIAL REIGN (19:11 – 20)

- (1) Before it (19:11 - 20:3)
- (2) During it (20:4-6)
- (3) After it (20:7-15)

2. THE ETERNAL STATE (21 – 22:5)

- (1) Descent of the city (21:1-8)
- (2) Description of the city (21:9-21)
- (3) Delights of the city (21:22 —— 22:5)

EPILOGUE (22:6-21)

- (a) Words of Comfort (6-17)
- (b) Words of Caution (18-21)